Improving Library Services to People with Disabilities

CHANDOS
INFORMATION PROFESSIONAL SERIES

Series Editor: Ruth Rikowski
(email: Rikowskigr@aol.com)

Chandos' new series of books are aimed at the busy information professional. They have been specially commissioned to provide the reader with an authoritative view of current thinking. They are designed to provide easy-to-read and (most importantly) practical coverage of topics that are of interest to librarians and other information professionals. If you would like a full listing of current and forthcoming titles, please visit our web site **www.chandospublishing.com** or contact Hannah Grace-Williams on email info@chandospublishing.com or telephone number +44 (0) 1865 884447.

New authors: we are always pleased to receive ideas for new titles; if you would like to write a book for Chandos, please contact Dr Glyn Jones on email gjones@chandospublishing.com or telephone number +44 (0) 1865 884447.

Bulk orders: some organisations buy a number of copies of our books. If you are interested in doing this, we would be pleased to discuss a discount. Please contact Hannah Grace-Williams on email info@chandospublishing.com or telephone number +44 (0) 1865 884447.

Improving Library Services to People with Disabilities

EDITED BY
COURTNEY DEINES-JONES

Chandos Publishing
Oxford · England

Chandos Publishing (Oxford) Limited
Chandos House
5 & 6 Steadys Lane
Stanton Harcourt
Oxford OX29 5RL
UK
Tel: +44 (0) 1865 884447 Fax: +44 (0) 1865 884448
Email: info@chandospublishing.com
www.chandospublishing.com

First published in Great Britain in 2007

ISBN:
978 1 84334 286 1 (paperback)
978 1 84334 287 8 (hardback)
1 84334 286 3 (paperback)
1 84334 287 1 (hardback)

Typeset by Domex e-Data Pvt. Ltd.
Printed in the UK and USA.

Contents

List of figures

Foreword

I believe that blind people like me are almost surreally naive, almost living in a parallel universe. We know the language of 'the sky is blue', 'the girl is beautiful', 'the stars are bright' and 'he looks threatening' but what do these really mean to us outside the necessary language of superficial discourse? We know that human beings are shown killing each other on the nightly news and in our crime thrillers but we do not know whether the inability to see this makes us less or more callous. We know that commodities are sold through sex but we do not know whether the deprivation from the ubiquity of sexual imagery makes us more or less able to have effective relations with our partners. We know how we are deprived of incalculable quantities of casual, serendipitous visual data with which our peers are bombarded but we do not know whether its absence makes us more thoughtful or more ignorant, or perhaps both. Depending on structure as we must, to help us make sense of the world, we do not know how well we understand a world which is increasingly improvisatory, aleatoric. We, who cannot step out of the door without planning, are thought years away from the casual freedom of our friends.

This is not the sort of language that you expect to hear from the visually impaired person (VIP) campaigner, from the lobbyist, from the ideological egalitarian; but if we do not understand how to face these questions honestly, we will suffer from an even wider gulf between ourselves and the rest of society.

Unless blind and visually impaired people are prepared to discuss and understand the depth of their deprivation, society will be severely limited in its capacity to provide sensitive facilitation. As usual, it is not the technology but the people who constitute the main barrier to solving our content accessibility problems and, not for the first time, the beneficiaries are a greater obstacle to progress than the providers.

At a level which is difficult to gauge, we have been in a state of denial, both librarians heroically being content providers with hopelessly low budgets and outputs compared with the world of print and pictures on the one hand, and VIP users bravely putting their notional equality ahead of their actual deprivation. The tact of the former and the vulnerability of the latter make it difficult to see how an honest dialogue can be commenced – but it must. We need help from people outside the sector, from authors, artists and engineers accustomed to designing and describing, people who come with no baggage, people who are not over-awed into denial by the gap between the real and the realised. These people should be brought in to teach us, not to substitute for us. After all, it is easy to write a list of what we each want other people to do, a list of outcomes for which we think somebody else should be responsible. But in the end, we – librarians and VIPs – have to take responsibility for ourselves and, above all, to know ourselves.

Kevin Carey
HumanITy

Preface

It is a great pleasure to be introducing this book providing international insight into services for people with disabilities. The book is designed for librarians, library users and people interested in promoting universal access to information. It is meant both to provide concrete strategies for service improvement and to give insight into how libraries might improve in reaching existing and potential patrons who have disabilities.

The beginning chapters address trends and strategies for improving access for people with specific disabilities. Atkinson and Dhiensa discuss how technology has improved access to information by people with print disabilities. Their discussion ranges from the development of Braille to uses of XML to provide more flexible alternative formats. Carey continues the theme with an incisive discussion of how technology trends are affecting information access for visually impaired persons. Technical and non-technical solutions to providing better service to deaf patrons are the focus of Allen's chapter. Tilley and her co-authors promote better access for people with physical disabilities. They demonstrate the growing importance of information and communications technology for information delivery and discuss ways in which libraries can improve information services.

The latter chapters more broadly address service improvements. Onatola uses Nigeria as an example of how libraries can provide better service. She addresses both the challenges faced by people wanting to improve library access in the face of indifference, and the potential that can be realised by facilitating universal access. Lee provides some guidance into how librarians can build initiatives to improve service, using the South Korean model as an example. I provide some suggestions for immediate ways by which librarians at all levels can improve service even when few resources are available. The volume concludes with Gottlieb's annotated bibliography and reference guide for information on service, library standards, funding and general disability resources.

Finally, a word on the compilation of this volume. In my experience, there is but a small community of librarians who combine a focus on disability access issues with the luxury of time and money needed to be active in conferences and activities. In short, we see the same handful of people, year after year. When agreeing to undertake this book, my first thought was to approach people from among this cohort and ask them to address specific chapters. Instead, I opted to put out general calls for writers, to provide the broadest perspective possible. The response was heartening, and the number of people willing – eager, in fact – to write on this topic gives me hope that the number of people in the rooms at IFLA and the virtual rooms on our professional exchanges will grow. I want to thank each of the contributing authors for their insight, their research and writing, and their patience.

Courtney Deines-Jones
The Grimalkin Group, LLC, Silver Spring MD

About the contributors

Mary Beth Allen is the Applied Health Sciences Librarian and Associate Professor of Library Administration at the University of Illinois at Urbana-Champaign, Illinois. She received a BA in Sociology, an MA in Teaching English as an International Language, and an MS in Library and Information Science, all from the University of Illinois at Urbana-Champaign. Her responsibilities in the Applied Health Sciences Library include building collections for and providing liaison and services to the departments of Speech and Hearing Science; Kinesiology and Community Health; Recreation, Sport and Tourism; and Disability Resources and Education Services.

Matthew Tylee Atkinson is a doctoral student in the Research School of Informatics at Loughborough University. His work is focused on making information systems, from computer games to websites, more accessible to their users. While Mr Atkinson is currently using vision impairment as a benchmark, many of the techniques he is helping develop will make information access easier for all. A relevant aspect of this work is 'Essentiality Tracks', a system for improving access to both websites and large, mainly procedure/technically-oriented documents.

Christine Susan Bruce is Associate Professor in the Faculty of Information Technology at Queensland University of

Technology. For the last five years there, she has been Director and Assistant Dean, Teaching and Learning. Her research interests revolve around the perceptual worlds of information and technology users. Her recent work has focused on information literacy, teaching and learning in higher education, community information use, and the collective consciousness of IT professionals and researchers.

Kevin Carey is the Founder Director of humanITy, a not-for-profit consultancy in e-inclusion, promoting universal access to electronic information. Mr Carey is Vice Chair of the Royal National Institute of the Blind and former Trustee of the National Library for the Blind, and combines his IT and library expertise with 15 years of work in over 70 developing countries. A graduate of Cambridge and Harvard, Mr Carey has published more than 100 papers on IT and inclusion. He also is a regular contributor to *Managing Information and Ability Magazine.*

Courtney Deines-Jones is Principal and Founder of The Grimalkin Group, LLC, a consulting firm specialising in finding everyday, common-sense ways to promote universal access to library services. Prior to forming her own business, she served as a public librarian and as head of a special library on disability and rehabilitation. Ms Deines-Jones is active in the American Library Association and IFLA, and has been published widely in the area of services to people who have disabilities. Ms Deines-Jones received her MLIS from Louisiana State University.

Jatinder Dhiensa is a full-time PhD researcher in e-accessibility for people with visual impairments. Her background is in the history and theory of art. However, she completed a Masters in Information Technology at Loughborough University during the Internet boom years. This ignited an interest in Internet accessibility, for which she returned to Loughborough

University to commence on a PhD in the field. Ms Dhiensa is member of ACM SIGACESS and IADIS, and has written and presented a number of publications.

Laura Roberts Gottlieb is in the Masters of Library Science programme at the College of Information Studies, University of Maryland, where she specialises in school library media. In addition to her current studies, Ms Gottlieb works for the Anne Arundel County Public Library system. Prior to pursuing her MLS, Ms Gottlieb worked in academic publishing as an American history acquisitions editor.

Gillian Hallam is an Associate Professor in the School of Information Systems at the Queensland University of Technology, coordinating the library and information management courses. Her academic activities have included QUT Teaching Fellow, CAVAL Visiting Scholar, and Fellow of the Higher Education Research and Development Association of Australasia. In 2004–05, Dr Hallam served as President of the Australian Library and Information Association. She has a deep interest in professional development and career-long learning, and is currently leading a major workforce planning study for the library and information sector in Australia.

Youngsook Lee is Librarian at the National Library of Korea in Seoul, South Korea, focusing on services to people with disabilities. In 2003, she led the move to establish the National Support Center of Library Services to People with Disabilities. Dr Lee is active in the Korean Library Association and IFLA. She has made numerous presentations on services to patrons who have disabilities. Dr Lee earned her PhD from the School of Library, Archive and Information Studies, University College London, University of London.

Ayo Onatola is Librarian, St. Christopher Iba Mar Diop College of Medicine, Luton. Formerly, he was Librarian,

Medical Schools and Teaching Hospitals of Ogun State (now Olabisi Onabanjo) University, Sagamu and Lagos State University, Ikeja. He earned his MLS from the University of Ibadan and is Member, Nigerian Library Association and Associate Member, Chartered Institute of Librarians and Information Professionals, UK. Mr Onatola's publications include *Basics of Librarianship – Theory and Practice: A Guide for Beginners*, published in 2004. Mr Onatola also regularly contributes to online and print librarianship journals.

Christine M. Tilley is a librarian with extensive experience in disability issues. Dr Tilley received her PhD in 2006 from Queensland University of Technology with her thesis titled 'A sense of control: A model of a virtual community for people with mobility disabilities'. She has lectured at QUT and other tertiary institutions and has served as an advisor and board member for numerous library and informational technology committees. An active member of the Australian Library and Information Association and Affiliate of the International Information Management Congress, Dr Tilley is also active in the Physical Disability Council of Australia Ltd. and other community organisations.

The contributors may be contacted via the editor:

Courtney Deines-Jones
Principal and Founder
The Grimalkin Group, LLC
8639B 16th St., #148
Silver Spring, MD 20910
USA

Tel: +1 240 462 8426
Fax: +1 301 587 6089
E-mail: *cdeinesj@grimalkingroup.com*

Improving library services to people with print disabilities: the role of technology in public libraries

Matthew Tylee Atkinson and Jatinder Dhiensa

Introduction

Traditionally, the term 'library' refers to a collection of books and journals. However, the ready availability of books, journals, papers, maps, artwork and other formats in libraries today allows the user to access a vast amount of information. This is further increased by electronic technologies that enable information to be stored in a range of formats. In this respect, the library is a tremendous source of information. Public libraries are the primary source for information queries from users with disabilities. To ensure that they can continue to provide this function, librarians must constantly address both the barriers that people with disabilities face when accessing information and the tools available to help people overcome these barriers.

Background

Public libraries have a long tradition of providing services to disabled people. In 1857, one of the first organisations to provide books for blind users was Liverpool's public library. Two decades later, alternative embossed formats including Braille were made available in public libraries. As a counterpoint, services to housebound individuals became available only after the Second World War. Hence, it can be suggested that different formats were available for disabled users well before accessibility to the material became a mainstream issue.

Print disability defined

> Disability: (n) A disadvantage or deficiency, especially a physical or mental impairment that interferes with or prevents normal achievement in a particular area.

To understand the concept of disability, it is of prime importance to first define the terminology used. Generally people are confused by the terms *impairment*, *disability* and *handicap* and often use them interchangeably. The World Health Organization (WHO) originally produced a classification of the terms in the form of the International Classification of Impairments, Disabilities and Handicaps (the three key words in the name have since been replaced by the less politically charged 'functioning, disability and health'):

- *Impairment* is a deviation from the generally accepted norm of the body function and structure as a result of a loss or abnormality. The 'body function' defines the physiological and psychological functions of the body. The 'body structure' includes the limbs and organs.

- *Disability* describes the inability to perform daily tasks and activities as a result of impairment.

- *Handicap* defines the social disadvantages to a person as a result of an impairment or disability. The term stems from the 'hostile social environment' suffered by a person with a disability. Because of numerous negative historical connotations, however, the term 'handicap' is not readily used.

Thus, persons with a print disability are those who are unable to perform the daily task or activity of reading standard print materials. These people would have an impairment preventing the use of standard print.

It can be argued that to identify one particular type of disability and to discuss the common requirements may lead to pigeonholing and negating other important factors. However, print disability focuses on resolving issues related to the disability, and as such does not make assumptions about underlying impairments. In literature, users with sensory impairments (i.e. visual impairments), other physical impairments, and cognitive impairments such as dyslexia are identified as users who have difficulty with traditional print. Their numbers are significant – for example, dyslexia affects some 4–10% of the UK population (James and Litterick, 2004).

Traditional print and disability: the international situation

As people get older, they are more likely to have a disability. Visual impairments represent the greatest disability group and the group that, as a whole, most needs alternatives to traditional print. WHO estimates that in 2002 there were 161 million people with visual impairments, of whom 37 million were blind. The organisation projects that by 2020 this number will have increased to 76 million. That amounts to a possible 76 million people who will not be able to use traditional print – excluding people who cannot use standard print for reasons other than visual impairment. For this reason, it is essential to make information available in different formats and to ensure that both current and potential library users are included.

Alternative formats

Libraries were originally places that stored physical materials, mainly books and journals. Now most libraries, especially public libraries, provide a one-stop shop for information contained in a multitude of formats ranging from traditional print books to CD-ROMs, printed journals, online journals, and others.

People who could not use traditional print can use many of the electronic resources now available, and alternative formats have been developed to facilitate access to print materials. The following sections describe three of the main alternatives to standard print.

Braille

Braille is a form of tactile communication used mainly by people who are blind or have very low vision (Dotless Braille, year unknown). It was developed in 1829 by Louis Braille, a young Frenchman, aged 20 (Hedge, 2006). Braille had been accidentally blinded at the age of three and attended a school for blind children in Paris. At the age of 11 he was introduced to a tactile code developed to allow soldiers to communicate in dark or smoky conditions. The code was based on a twelve-dot cell, two dots wide by six dots high. A combination of dots stood for a letter or a sound. Braille adapted the code and, by reducing cell size from twelve to six, enabled the fingertip to encompass the cell completely. This allowed the reader to gain an impression of one cell and then quickly move to the next. Braille continued to refine his writing system until his death.

Today, Braille has two different meanings. It can either refer to a Braille alphabet, a set of characters or cells designed for reading by touch, or to one of the many Braille codes. Sixty-four unique dot combinations are possible with a six-dot Braille cell, where one particular combination is blank and is used as a space (see, for example, Figure 1.1; braillecode.com, year unknown). Braille symbols are a Braille cell or a sequence of Braille cells that have a single meaning. An example of a Braille symbol is two cells that create an uppercase letter. Braille dot patterns are the arrangements of dots that make up a particular cell. The most commonly used method of describing a dot pattern is to list the position numbers of the dots. Extended Braille character sets frequently use eight dots. A single eight-dot cell can be used to replace a standard two-cell symbol. Another example of an extended Braille character set is the Dot Plus that uses either six or eight-dot cells as well as other tactile symbols.

Braille cells have no universal meaning. The meaning depends upon the particular Braille code and the local context in which it is being used. Braille codes are described

Figure 1.1 Example of letters in standard Braille, formed by a combination of six raised dots

as 'elegant, concise and very human systems' used for transcribing printed material using a Braille alphabet. Braille codes are similar to computer codes as they are 'a system of symbols given certain arbitrary meanings and used for transmitting messages requiring brevity.'

Historically, Braille has been written using a stylus and slate or on a typewriter-like machine called a Brailler, which has six keys representing each dot in the cell. This in itself can be restricting as it cannot produce eight-cell or extended Braille. Today, people also can use computers to produce Braille.

Barriers to Braille use include the time needed to learn the code; age-related decreases in fingertip sensitivity that can make it hard for older people to read Braille; and a lack of available Braille materials, especially in developing nations. Hence, not all people who are blind or have serious visual impairments use Braille. Instead, they rely on a range of assistive technologies, from talking books and screen readers to screen magnification.

Talking books

Audio outputs in the form of recorded or synthesised speech have made it easier for people with print disabilities of all kinds to access information. Prior to the invention of synthesised speech, audio recordings, large print and Braille books were the only method for the visually-impaired to access reading materials. Producing each translation was time-consuming and impractical for many ephemeral or special interest materials.

However, this changed with the development of synthesised speech. While synthetic speech has been available for some time, the transition to digital information gives it even more promise. The Digital Accessible

Information System (DAISY) is a standard format that breaks down text into chunks and uses screen reading software to read the words on the computer screen.

A DAISY book can be explained as a set of digital files that include:

- one or more digital audio files containing a human narration of part or all of the source text;

- a marked-up file containing some or all of the text (strictly speaking, this marked-up text file is optional);

- a synchronisation file to relate markings in the text file with time points in the audio file; and

- a navigation control file which enables the user to move smoothly between files while synchronisation between text and audio is maintained.

The DAISY standard allows the producing agency full flexibility regarding the mix of text and audio, ranging from audio-only, to full-text and audio, to text-only.

There are 14 Full Members of the DAISY Consortium, more than 55 Associate Members, and more than 20 Friends.

- Full and Associate Members are nonprofit organisations, typically national talking book libraries or national consortia of such libraries.

- Friends are for-profit organisations including developers of production and/or playback hardware or software (DAISY Consortium, 2006).

When incorporated into computer software, DAISY enables users to scan books and have them read back to them by a synthesised or recorded human voice. The user is able to adjust the speed at which the text is read out, to place bookmarks and to move forwards or backwards through chapters at a touch of a button.

Electronic materials

The digital age has seen a transition from traditional print, large print and embossed formats to electronic methods of accessing information. Electronic access ranges from access to the Internet, CD-ROMs, online journals and e-Books, e-Music and other online services. Many public libraries now offer portals that users can search for e-Books. They can download the results and read them using a screen reader, output them to a refreshable Braille display, or have them read at leisure.

Reference materials also are available in electronic format. The importance of having dictionaries, thesauri, encyclopaedias and other materials available online is highlighted by James and Litterick.[1] They believe that by conducting computer-based searches, users will not have to worry about the spelling of words (which is a problem faced by some users with dyslexia) and will be able to traverse many documents and media sources with a single search, retrieving more and more relevant information.

Technology adoption – the accessibility cycle

Many mainstream technologies are developed for the 'average' person. Being mostly usable by most people can go a long way to ensuring success in the marketplace. Unfortunately, the needs of people with disabilities often are not average – and there are inevitably some technologies they cannot access.

There are two common ways to get around this problem: retrofitting technology and using adaptive technologies to make otherwise inaccessible information available.

Retrofitting

The most common approach is retrofitting some form of accessibility system on top of the mainstream technology. This often exposes most of the essential functions of the underlying technology but frequently limits the scope of what the disabled person can achieve due to assumptions made during its design (for example, the 'accessible' digital radio, with buttons that can be easily used, but which is unable to read out text sent from the radio station to the blind user).

By retrofitting an existing mainstream technology, it can be kept current and made accessible to a wider audience of users. Though there are some significant disadvantages to this method (which will be discussed later), it can be the most effective and easy-to-implement approach in some situations. In many countries and jurisdictions there is a legal requirement for some technologies to be made accessible, so retrofitting is a common practice. Large organisations favour it because it enables them to continue using the toolset and processes they currently employ. Development of accessibility improvements is usually considered when the user base of a given technology, such as the print book, personal computer or World Wide Web, reaches a critical mass. The effect of this is that there can be a significant time lag before a system is rendered accessible to users with disabilities. As the technology eventually becomes obsolete and is replaced by newer versions, most users can move on, but people with disabilities often have to wait because the new technology is not yet accessible. Moore's graph of technology adoption demonstrates the lags involved for people with disabilities (Figure 1.2).

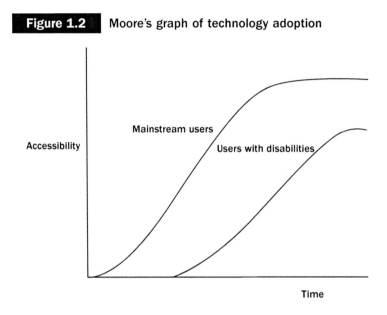

Figure 1.2 Moore's graph of technology adoption

Using adaptive technologies for print materials

There are alternative physical media to standard print. These include large print, Braille and talking/audio books. Their advantage is that no extra equipment is necessary to adapt them to their target users. Their disadvantage is that they can be expensive to produce.

To augment these alternatives, a range of solutions is available to enable access to print material. Most of them can be effective, especially when a library has a large number of patrons who could make use of such technology and/or access is sought for general reading material. If, however, more specialist access is required, less traditional methods may need to be used.

Many users may be able to access traditional print material through the use of extra equipment. A large range of such support equipment exists, with great variation in terms of technology level, cost and effectiveness for given groups of people. Examples include:

- coloured films placed over the printed page may enable some dyslexic patrons to read the text;
- simple lens magnifiers can help moderately vision-impaired people decipher text;
- CCTV-based magnification devices are suited for stronger vision impairments due to the range of magnification and image manipulation options on offer;
- scan-to-speech systems – either dedicated hardware devices or a combination of optical character recognition (OCR), text-to-speech (TTS) and/or screen magnification software – provide multiple options and are suitable for people with a broad range of print disabilities;
- electronic file delivery in a flat ASCII (or Unicode) format allows users who have their own adaptive computer systems to use the output method they prefer.

An important trend to note, which also applies in other areas of accessibility, is that as we move down the list of devices above, the cost and complexity increases, they target users who are further from being able to access printed material and their effectiveness in specialist situations can be reduced.

Though these limitations may not be a problem in some general areas and the cost of high-technology solutions could be justified by numbers of patrons willing to use them, they may still not be appropriate. For example, taking the example of a newspaper, consider low-vision readers, familiar with the page-layout concepts used by newspapers, who want to read a newspaper that is not available electronically. We can surmise that some form of magnification would enable these patrons to access the material almost as effectively as their sighted counterparts.

They are familiar with the flow of text on the page and most will be able to benefit from the inclusion of images. However, a user who must convert the printed articles to Braille text or speech could have great problems, even with the newest technologies. OCR software is improving at recognising the layout of pages, particularly when only two or three columns are used and the input material is of high quality. Unfortunately, the bridging of OCR and text-to-speech technology is not currently as successful and often results in errors being introduced. It is quite common for such systems to read across columns and captions for figures, rather than down columns. It is also important to note that figures, illustrations and advertisements are almost certainly inaccessible to the reader and, as the medium is aimed at sighted people, no alternative textual description is provided. In addition, in the case of specialist publications, particularly scientific or mathematical ones that contain formulae, the scan-to-speech solution is almost useless due to the lack of technology to convert mathematical equations into an accessible form.

It is important to bear in mind that this area is an example of a very common trend: the more 'bridging' a retrofitted access technology has to do, the more likely it is to be complex, costly and effective only in general areas. It is quite possible it could be of great use, but this depends upon the size and nature of the intended user-base.

Adapting electronic information

Many people assume that electronic information, by its inherent nature, will be universally accessible. There are good reasons why this should be the case, but all too often it is not. In this section, we have selected three popular formats and explain how their usability, accessibility and potential legal issues interact. The important thing to note is that although these are specific technological examples, the situations they typify are common and can be more broadly applied.

PDF

The Portable Document Format, used extensively by the publishing industry, is a close electronic match to printed material. As an electronic format, it can be magnified and manipulated to a certain extent. However, problems inherent in how PDF is designed prevent most print-disabled people from using it effectively (Mazrui, 2005):

- Vision-impaired users who already use screen magnification to view the computer must cope with two independent levels of zooming and panning on the screen. The access software shows only a portion of the entire screen on the monitor; panning is used to view the rest of the image. In a PDF-viewing application, zooming may be used to show a given area of the page at once, with scrolling features to move about the (virtual) page. A screen magnifier user would have to accommodate both of these levels of zooming and panning – a cumbersome and somewhat tiring activity.

- As PDFs use what are essentially line and curve drawing instructions to render the text and many graphical elements, they are not recognisable as text by screen readers. This means that people who rely on text-to-speech software will not be able to access most PDFs. A large number of PDFs are created by scanning in a printed work as a series of images. Naturally, these suffer from similar accessibility problems as well as a general loss in quality compared with documents initially created electronically.

- Due to digital rights management and other edit and copy-protection measures incorporated into many PDFs, there are few workarounds (such as 'copy and pasting' into a Text-To-Speech system) that could be used to extract textual content and increase accessibility of these documents, even when the material is coded as text.

Fortunately, some of these drawbacks are being addressed. One driving force is that some governments are searching for an open standard format for information dissemination to the general public, and PDF currently seems to be the de facto standard. Developments such as 'tagging' (where textual content is included in such a way that screen readers may access it) are improving accessibility somewhat, but they still suffer from layout issues and the fact that awareness about such problems is very low.

This example goes to further demonstrate the points made above in relation to how the adoption of some seemingly new technologies can cause accessibility barriers to increase, especially when stemming from a former use in areas where accessibility was not a concern – in this example, the use of PostScript technology (upon which PDF is based) in the publishing and printing industries.

PDF is an example of an electronic format that poses as many accessibility challenges as its physical counterpart. By forcing the use of traditional metaphors (such as the breaking of documents into pages), we negate the potential of computer systems to help us locate and present information in the way that is most suited to each individual patron.

Plain text

In terms of accessibility, the plain text document can be seen as the opposite of PDF. It is a format that lacks almost all methods for providing formatting, graphics, pagination, predictable or fixed wrapping of lines and other contemporary design techniques. All of these qualities make it an excellent format for presenting information accessibly to vision-impaired and particularly blind patrons. Users can choose which font, colours and/or Braille translation method is most appropriate to them. They can search for text and reformat the document to ensure lines are of an acceptable width if they so desire.

Many of these same qualities, however, are the well-established reasons for plain text not being a mainstream format for disseminating information. The lack of images, security and authenticity of information, and concerns about illegal distribution are the principal issues for most authors.

Web-based formats – HTML and XML

Unlike other formats for dissemination, information provided on the Internet (in this example we discuss formats such as HTML and XML) is often freely available and in many cases does not attempt to remain analogous to paper-based material. Key implications of this are that text size and layout are more fluid, and documents can easily encompass many different modalities (including text, sound, video, images and interactive elements). Further, information from disparate sources is easily searchable; documents in related areas are often densely linked and information is often changing and being updated.

Based on the discussion above, most of these qualities may seem ideal for both 'average' users and people with print disabilities. However, while there is great potential for improvement in the future, there are currently two especially serious barriers to accessibility:

- Many sites are designed poorly, using deprecated design techniques, platform-specific conventions and complicated or inconsistent layout and navigation schemes. These issues affect everyone but significantly increase the time it takes for people using adaptive technologies to find the information that they are looking for.

- A growing number of sites now require the use of 'plug-ins' to view content – content that in most cases could have been easily created using techniques compliant with web development standards. When non-standard methods of presenting content are used, the chance that a presentation is accessible decreases significantly. The use of animations, video and some types of 'applet' technology almost ensure that a person using adaptive technologies will be excluded from using a given site.

These main issues also cause problems for 'average' users of sites, especially those who are accessing the site by means other than a standard computer (such as via a mobile telephone or PDA). A recent report by the UK Disability Rights Commission (2004) shows that websites are 35 per cent easier to use for *everyone* if they are accessible to people who have disabilities (i.e. compliant with accessibility (W3C, 1999) and other web standards). This tells us that accessibility is a valid metric by which we can estimate the usability of websites for *all* people.

By extension, through compliance with web development standards, libraries should be able to improve the productivity of all people wishing to access their website and web-based documents – documents created in a format that can be displayed readily by web browsers (i.e. HTML, XML, but not PDF as this requires a 'plug-in'). A large number of software manuals, lecture notes, product leaflets, government information packs and so on fall under this category.

Fortunately, significant interest has been generated recently in ensuring that websites are made accessible for their users. Some countries have created new legislation to encourage this, as mentioned above. Given this, it is interesting to note that a vast percentage of government websites are still inaccessible (BBC, 2006).

With the trend towards gradually increasing accessibility of websites, it is important to bear in mind that this area could have a dramatic impact on the accessibility of library services for patrons with print disabilities. It is imperative that existing sites be checked for accessibility problems and new sites be designed to avoid such problems. Because people with print disabilities may also have impairments that make coming to the library in person more difficult, providing accessible web-based information can greatly increase library use by this community. Conversely, excluding these patrons from the website may exclude them from the library as a whole.

There are many tools on offer – a significant number of these being free and open for everyone to use – to assess the accessibility of websites and give feedback on how this can be improved. A discussion of the particulars is out of the scope of this work, but the fact that web accessibility does not have to be a large burden to the competent web designer is an important one to note.

A number of technologies are under development to enable users to be presented with information that is more relevant to their needs and in the formats they prefer (Dhiensa et al., 2005; Atkinson et al., 2006). These tools, if brought into the mainstream could dramatically improve the accessibility – really usability, as we are concerned with all users – of web-based documents. The ideas of 'essentiality and proficiency' and the associated tools for users and authors of documents provide a standard to which the importance (essentiality) of information in a document can be marked-up. Subsequently the document can be displayed according to the user's preferences for essentiality of information and according to the nature of the device (telephone, PDA, computer) or disability they may have.

Future trends – a better way

> Always remember that you are unique. Just like everyone else. (Unknown)

An ideal electronic format would exhibit similar qualities to the text file – mutability and presenting minimal accessibility issues. Such properties would be beneficial for all users. The format also would have to incorporate the ability to present images and a pleasing design for non-print-disabled users. Everyone would wish to use such a format, and it would eliminate segregating patrons with specific needs.

Sometimes, in developing a retrofit accessibility solution, a format that could be better for everyone emerges, as the DAISY example illustrates. Unfortunately, such positive (potentially for us all) developments are often overlooked or ignored. The main reasons for this are that such technologies are seen as 'for disabled people' – if people are aware of them at all – and (probably the most significant reason) an industry that has already adopted one format is naturally reluctant to invest in moving to a new one. This is true even if that new format promises higher productivity than the current one. Companies also have an economic interest in promulgating proprietary formats rather than embracing open source solutions that can be used and modified by all.

Belief that making materials accessible to people with print disabilities will benefit only a small niche audience is why retrofitting is often employed. We believe that in the future, a better argument will be used more often: that designing a format that is flexible for us all to use and benefit from is desirable for the vast numbers of 'average' users and is the best way. By taking advantage of both our similarities and differences, we will be much more productive than by insisting everyone adopts the average format for the average person.

Supporting this goal, there is a growing interest in the academic sector in providing interfaces to systems that can adapt to meet the requirements of their users (Iaccarino et al., 2006; Arrue et al., 2006). The central requirement for a system to be able to achieve this is that the information processing it carries out must be separate to the way the output is rendered – so that, for example, the user could use sight, touch or sound to interact with the system.

An example from the publishing world is the DocBook XML standard for writing technical documentation (though it has been applied in much wider areas). It promotes the separation of content from style, much as accessible web standards do. Thus, once the document has been authored, it can be displayed automatically in many different formats – from PDF to HTML to plain text. This makes it highly suitable for both patrons with disabilities using adaptive technology and 'average' users who may want to access the document in a variety of different situations, using a range of devices. Work is ongoing to incorporate the ideas of essentiality and proficiency into DocBook XML and to generalise them further so that essentiality can be specified based on the role that a given user has each time he or she accesses a document.

Conclusion

Those providing library services will be aware of the current challenges involved in helping people who have print disabilities find information that they require, in an acceptable format. The challenges and solutions discussed here could be thought of as a generalisation of those problems. Though formats come and go, the fundamental issues are often strikingly similar. In the future, many of the now prominent challenges should be overcome, but the need for increased awareness and promotion of inclusive standards that benefit us all will remain.

Note

1. See, for example UK Disability Discrimination Act 2005 (*http://www.opsi.gov.uk/acts/acts2005/20050013.htm*) and the US Rehabilitation Act 1973, as amended, s. 508, *http://www .access-board.gov/sec508/guide/act.htm*.

2

Library services to people with special needs: a discussion of blind and visually impaired people as an exemplar

Kevin Carey

Alternative format production and libraries

Unlike a general commentary on standard print library services where the supply of material for loan, as set against the supply of material published, can be taken for granted, any commentary on the history and present status of library services for visually impaired persons (VIPs) would be incomplete without some consideration of alternative format publishing and production. Whereas the task of the print librarian is to analyse publishers' lists of books, periodicals and journals to see which fraction of the whole oeuvre best fits the purpose and budget of a particular library, the alternative format librarian is reluctant to reject any material immediately available, and in most places will also have the task of deciding which of the mass of printed material available should be rendered in alternative formats. For this reason, it is impossible to separate production and availability.

Librarians should be aware of the potential importance of producing digital multimedia suitable for:

- adults with learning difficulties – primarily through the use of automated simplification tools (too often such people are given children's material);

- deaf people – through adding subtitles to audio multimedia;

- people with physical disabilities – through embedding metadata into electronic files that allow the use of binary switches;

- blind people – through the addition of audio and video description to multimedia.

The primary focus of this chapter is access by VIPs. This has historically been the focus of alternative format media, and serves as an exemplar of the wider field.

The Royal National Institute of the Blind (RNIB) estimates[1] that approximately 4 per cent of books published in the UK are rendered in alternative formats (primarily audio). So little other material (periodicals, magazines, journals etc.) is rendered that it corrects to 0 per cent. A brief survey of the Organisation for Economic Cooperation and Development (OECD) countries reveals that the UK performs better than all except perhaps Canada, which produces a slightly higher percentage of its modest indigenous output. Production in all other countries corrects to 0 per cent.

The selection criteria in OECD countries which produce alternative format materials may be conveniently, though not entirely tidily, split into three types:

- popular works of fiction and biography for general readers;

- 'classic' fiction and non-fiction whose contemporaneously perceived virtues justify immediate incorporation;

- ad hoc rendering in response to individual needs, mostly in connection with formal education.

Developing country material is almost entirely confined to the last category.

With the possible exception of contemporary light fiction, OECD and all other national holdings fall short in every category, and particularly with respect to:

- contemporary, as opposed to outdated, academic material, especially in subjects which are incorrectly thought to change very little over time, such as philosophy and theology;
- popularising non-fiction and lifestyle material frequently based on public service broadcasting;
- fiction falling outside bestseller lists and light genre fiction;
- ephemera;
- pornography (the production of a Braille version of Playboy in the USA was short-lived).

Scarcity and a production lag between print and alternative format of up to two years have been constant negative factors in access. These were understandable when very different production techniques were used for audio, modified print and Braille. But during the first quarter century of the digital age, when convergences in production have become simple, the impact of computing on producing Braille, modified print and synthetic speech has been surprisingly small. There are five reasons for this, which apply in different degrees in different places:

- The continuing management of Braille production systems on traditional, 'sheltered workshop' lines with only minor changes in production practice between analogue and digital (notably in the failure to use electronic tools for quality control). Also compromising this system is a genuine tension between the employment of VIP adults and the material needs of blind children.

- An unbalanced emphasis, often as the result of misguided lobbying, on automated Braille translation software coding which is reliable, as opposed to layout, which requires human mediation.

- A false perception that one must decide between producing Braille and large print from a single, digital file, rather than using the single file to produce multiple alternative formats.

- The almost complete dismissal of synthetic speech production.

- Mythological economics that underestimate the cost of mechanical (analogue) production and over-estimate the cost of digital production.

The analogue/digital factor provides an easy example. The advantages of digital over analogue production include:

- lower overheads, cheaper equipment, lower labour costs per unit of output;

- cheaper error correction where the differential widens in proportion to required accuracy;

- cheaper distribution and duplication;

- format flexibility among Braille, synthetic speech and different formats of modified print.

Nonetheless, many systems continue to adhere to analogue production using the argument that digital is too expensive.

The National Association for the Blind facility in Mumbai and African Braille Computer Development (ABCD) in Nairobi have both demonstrated that high-quality alternative format files in a variety of languages can be produced outside the OECD. With a little training it is perfectly possible for librarians to produce modified print[2] and synthetic speech files from digital sources and it is even possible for them to produce Braille from relatively straightforward files (plain text in a single language with few layout complexities).

One final remark may help to explain the imbalance of output between Braille and modified print where the potential demand for the latter is much greater. Organisations that serve VIPs tend, quite properly, to take account of the views of users. Not only in the West, but all over the world, the vocal user community that contributes most to policy formulation consists of the tiny minority of congenitally or paediatrically blind people who have grown up in the visual impairment education system as Braille users, as opposed to both to children with residual vision and adventitiously blind people who are highly resistant to Braille and require modified print and/or audio.

This result of this bias is the availability of lot of audio and some commercial large print, but a focus by major producers for blind and visually impaired people on investing the bulk of their budgets into Braille, and hardly any into large print. This is even more true for developing country production (*vide* Tanzania, Zambia, Ethiopia, Ghana, Paraguay, Sri Lanka, Fiji), where African and Asian organisations of and for blind people have received Braille printing presses from overseas donors. This, incidentally, should warn those quite rightly concerned with user participation and feedback against an uncritical demographic and automatic acceptance of narrow consumer input.

The right to read, copyright and graphical information

The extent to which VIPs can access alternative format material is not only limited by the use of technology, it is also legally restricted. Nowhere is the right to read an absolute right and nowhere is a theoretical right to information translated into anything like complete enjoyment of a right. In spite of the fact that VIPs pay direct or sales taxes that contribute to public library services, this is no guarantee that they will receive any return for their payments. Further, public sector reluctance has been shored up by not-for-profit providers who have grown to see their client base as an institutional asset. As long as the private, voluntary sector is prepared to finance and provide a service, no matter how incomplete, the public sector will surely allow it.

Once public sector obligation and not-for-profit sector limitations have been fully clarified, the appropriate model is specialist providers as paid agents of the public sector. An important first step is to establish case law and regulations on what constitutes a library service and whether this does, or should, include provision for VIPs. Almost all library legislation makes an open commitment to 'all citizens' but this rarely reaches those who need special provision. Unfortunately, none of the major, wealthy not-for-profits in the OECD have fought a test case.

Copyright

Then there is copyright. The librarian should take a practical approach to this when thinking about alternative format provision. Two suggestions:

- find out what material is out of copyright or has never been in it; there are now massive and growing resources like Project Gutenberg, Wikipedia, and the BBC that provide electronic format materials free;

- check the law on fair use, which allows a certain amount of copying. It is important to know what length and number of extracts can be copied and how many copies can be made. In general, the 'fair use' provision will cover alternative format production for an individual reader.

There is a general principle that if a library buys a copy or pays for a lending right then it should be able to produce one alternative format copy without explicit permission, as the author cannot be shown to have been disadvantaged. One of the main reasons why alternative format copyright is in such a mess is that agencies have confused the right to produce with the right to produce without benefit to the author.

Too often publishers resist alternative format provision, particularly in the digital domain, because of an irrational conflation of music and pornography piracy with conventional print material.

While copyright most often is a barrier to alternative format production, it is important to highlight positive developments:

- public sector broadcasters are making multimedia content available for limited periods after broadcast – the international implications of this development should be pursued as a matter of urgency;
- broadcasters, universities, museums and companies are making huge amounts of archive multimedia available free or at low cost;
- analogue text libraries are being rapidly digitised – this makes an investment of time and money in 'file migration' extremely important.

Librarians can help by holding publishers accountable. Publishers should be forced to base their arguments on evidence and probability rather than fear and possibility; there is something incongruous in the picture of a totally blind person producing personal copies of nineteenth century novels when feature films are routinely pirated before official release. In addition, state-backed library services should consider ranking the rights of users above publishers, risking prosecution.

In addition, librarians are encouraged to adopt two much wider strategies, which, over time, will reduce this legal burden: libraries should work together to assemble a global digital deposit, and rights of access should be platform independent.

Graphical and multimedia information

Authorial integrity also has been a stated concern restricting alternative format production. Authors fear that by putting electronic files under someone else's control, design or content could be altered and their original intent lost.

It was the pursuit of authorial integrity that led to the development of the Portable Document Format (PDF). The very nature of PDF militated against accessibility. This was not so much in its presentation of the plain text but instead because of its promoting layout, metadata, epigraphia and subtext over the text itself. Its greater significance lies in its foreshadowing the migration from computerised symbolic language strings (from simple ASCII to complex HTML) to graphics formats. Other recent, growing examples include cameras in mobile telephones and downloading video from the Internet.

The implications of these developments are enormous for VIPs. While the sector is still struggling with the world of digital text, the global digital economy is becoming graphical. By 2010, private photographic files and commercial video will dwarf text production (including 20 million current blogging sites) on the Internet. This is HumanITy's very conservative estimate. One needs only to compare the file sizes of 1,000 words of print (25 KB), a digital photograph (1 MB) and a feature length film (2.5 GB) to see the difference. There is already a considerable move towards delivering feature films on demand over broadband and there is already a considerable amount of broadcasting beginning over broadband to avoid restrictions (such as those imposed by the FCC in the USA) that govern broadcasting over licence spectrum. This does not even consider the impact of voice over telephony.

To continue to provide information to VIPs, librarians and alternative format producers must learn from its problems in the age of digital text and:

- develop and own common tools to render text from graphics files into a form that can be turned into a source file, which in turn can produce alternative formats;
- develop common templates through which we can render these files;
- agree on metadata conventions for alternative format description;
- anticipate future developments.

The provision of multimedia content on the Internet is of particular importance to VIPs, people with hearing impairments or learning difficulties because the material is rich, combining moving pictures, audio and text and often subtitles and audio and video description. Librarians must be careful not to make a crude correlation between text and seriousness and multimedia and frivolity, and should work to make these materials known to and available by their visually impaired patrons.

The public and not-for-profit specialist sectors need to make deals with the producers of commercial multimedia, audio books and text archives; the parallel operations of the two sectors are wasteful.

The global library

Because of the low production of alternative format materials, the development of a truly global library is especially promising to VIPs. There are two basic requirements to achieve the global library: common (or at least derivable common) formats, and international copyright agreements.

Although we live in a world of global data networks and increasing interoperability, automation has not achieved what it should. The sector has incorrectly put its faith in printers' files that could be automatically rendered in alternative formats. Unfortunately, these are almost invariably application hybrids without style/content separation. They are rendered in a quasi-graphic format that does not lend itself to portability among platforms. Astonishingly, it is often quicker to scan and edit a printed novel from scratch than to use the electronic printer's file.

Currently, the best option for production by the sector and access to source material is through the use of pure HTML files. These can subsequently be rendered through style sheets to produce different formats. To achieve the global library ideal, specialist librarians will need to work with national libraries and, through them, with international companies and producers to establish and implement necessary standardisation.

As previously noted, progress also is needed with international copyright issues; this too must be achieved across platforms. There is little point in fighting a long battle for the right to reproduce a document in Braille if the same battle is then required for modified print, synthetic speech, real audio and every new medium that emerges. It will take much longer to achieve a generic right rather than a medium-based right of access, but the effort will be worthwhile.

Towards superfluity

It can be seen from the above that the problem of scarcity outlined in the first paragraph might soon be a problem of superfluity. This requires consideration of the following with reference to VIPs:

- navigation – finding information;
- evaluation – according weight and relevance to data;
- migration – making digital files accessible.

In the analogue age, the first two of these were librarian-led. The librarian decided how to catalogue (evaluation) and where to store (navigation) the book. The librarian also advised readers as to which books were best suited to their needs (navigation and evaluation). Books were usually in a fixed format so there were no migration possibilities.

Navigation

As librarians will appreciate, the key to efficient navigation is sound taxonomy. This is even more the case for VIPs who cannot rapidly scan vast arrays of classes of data. In the computer environment, screen readers cannot easily convey, either in voice or Braille display, the spatial aspects of data classification. Even where the metadata do not rely upon spatial clues, the choices offered are too many to be efficiently retained by a user who listens or touches exclusively one line at a time. As Moore's formulation shows, if the optimum number of choices in conducting a complex search is between 5 and 9 (7 ± 2) there has to be a complex trade-off between classes and 'clicks'. The larger the number of classes, the fewer the number of clicks, and vice versa. Many people overcome this problem by using Boolean search language to define their needs. This overcomes some of the problems of poor taxonomy, but depends on an accessible input device. VIPs may need tools such as:

- a Braille-like input device;
- a qwerty input device with voice feedback to verify entry;
- voice in (this is currently not reliable for extended use);
- SMS (more widely used than qwerty)
- on-screen customisation of the text input box.

Underlying the special problems of VIPs in the field of navigation, there is a deeper question – should we abandon our twentieth-century near obsession with metadata and rely much more heavily on teaching and learning how to define searches that trigger context-sensitive results? During the last 20 years, alternative format librarians have been fixated on metadata when there has only been limited data to classify. Paradoxically, with the advent of content superfluity we may simultaneously be leaving the age of metadata. Librarians will not be redundant because although people will want to search autonomously for some of the time, many will need the librarian to work with them on search strategies. In addition, because the librarian will be able to scan on-screen options and input to a text box, many VIPs will choose to moderate their autonomy in exchange for efficiency. In this context, librarians will need to adapt their methodology so that they can collaborate with the user rather than simply working autonomously 'on behalf' of a user.

Evaluation

Librarians rightly value their traditional, non-judgmental position as information arbiters; but they have been protected in this to a large degree by the relationship between the nature of material and its format. Books, peer-reviewed journals, periodicals, magazines, 'quality' and tabloid newspapers and, for that matter, self-publishing and private views, all commanded instant market recognition simply because they are presented in a highly identifiable format. Users largely assessed the kind of information they were offered according to its physical presentation. At a more profound level, there was, until quite recently, a set of firm cultural demarcations between, for example, fact and fiction; fact and comment; fact and advertising; peer review and self-publishing; publishing and broadcasting.

These links between physical presentation and content have become much weaker in the analogue world – and have largely disappeared in the digital world. Content evaluation has become much more difficult, but for VIPs, such judgments are inevitable and vital, if unwelcome. As content supply explodes, VIPs cannot hope to gain access to all of this material. Choices have to be made.

Traditionally, book selection for alternative format production has been a librarian's function in the context of a not-for-profit publishing and analogue Brailling/recording context. The output was intended either for a broad market or for a highly-specific educational purpose. Digital technology has lowered both the cost and the barriers between different alternative formats. At the same time, it has made production for small groups and individuals far more viable. This, in turn, changes the role of an accessible format librarian selector from being an institutional adviser to being an adviser to individuals.

General librarians also need to have some basic awareness of what can and cannot be adapted for use by VIPs. Common points are:

- VIPs access data more slowly than their seeing peers;
- speculative or serendipitous learning is much 'thinner' than that of seeing peers;
- alternative format production, though becoming cheaper, is much more expensive than standard production.

Acting autonomously when searching, VIPs also will suffer from many of the same problems as their seeing peers:

- their own limited knowledge in general;
- limited knowledge within their sector;
- presentation of results according to commercial content ranking (in Google, Yahoo etc);
- a tendency to use only what they reach first.

The librarian and the user must be clear about what the search and evaluation process is and use it consciously, rather than making assumptions that are not mutually understood. For a librarian to exercise a value judgment is somewhat 'counter cultural' but to draw back from this strategy will almost certainly damage the interests of clients. VIPs will only have a limited grasp of the wilder shores of the Web and will need help; this is equally so with broadcasting and multimedia.

Migration

Migration covers a mass of rendering issues. The most important are summarised in the sections below.

Description

The most important barrier to content migration is between the picture (as opposed to a technical diagram) and the text rendition. Even where the quality of description is high, there is always a gulf between a work of art and its catalogue description. This issue is further complicated by the different, more fundamental requirements, of congenitally and adventitiously blind people and those with residual vision.

Tools

The conversion of content between formats through the use of tools is a core strategy for migration. Currently, the key tools requirements are conversion between and among:

- word processing formats;
- word processing formats and HTML;
- Graphics files containing text and manipulable word processing formats;
- metadata and data customisation;
- layout conversion macros for modified print and Braille;
- legacy content migration (many VIPs have legacy operating systems, programmes and data).

All these aspects can be summarised in a simple rule: upgrade all material to your most advanced format.

Scale-usable display

When a page of text or an image is scaled up or down, this presents layout problems:

- with books, unless the layout metadata are separated from the data (style from content), items such as headers appear in the middle of pages;

- with text and images, gross magnification can cause a loss of orientation – there must always be a balance between magnification and orientation;
- in Braille transcription, the general assumption is that the central problem is print to Braille symbol conversion – this is not so; the key weakness of automated Braille translation software is its poor handling of layout and page making;
- Determining the scale of tactile diagrams involves a balance between fineness of detail and overall grasp.

Lexicality

Content layout does not always follow the traditional order of vertical and horizontal order. Current automated systems handle this problem poorly.

Information systems and convergence

The following sections summarise the characteristics of the Internet, broadcasting and telecommunications as they impinge upon library services for VIPs. Understanding their particular and joint implications to VIPs is essential to providing effective service in the digital age.

The Internet

Internet content is indescribably heterogeneous. For VIPs, whose information searching and processing is enforcedly deliberative, this presents both a major opportunity and a challenge. The opportunity is to lift VIP content access out of its traditionally narrow channel. This has traditionally limited outlook and made reading a largely conformist experience, largely dependent on institutionally mediated alternative format production and regulated broadcasting. The challenge is to direct content access towards the purpose for which it is required. The Internet, however, is in a state of transition from a largely textual to a largely multimedia carrier. Three major streams of data are carried in bulk on the Internet:

- commercial video on demand
- broadcasting;
- personal photography and video.

These are growing, and the providers of these streams of data, especially commercial video and broadcasting, will inevitably become dominant in defining Internet standards. Those standards are likely to be much more concerned with multimedia transmission and cost recovery than text accessibility.

Broadcasting

The age of linear television confined to transmitting on scarce spectrum allocated by governments is almost at an end. Linear television has already been complemented by video recording for time-shifted viewing (e.g. TiVo), now supplemented by video on demand from broadcasters and other commercial suppliers. Television costs are falling and even standard televisions can be linked to PCs to accept transmission or play files downloaded over the Internet. Internet broadcasting will circumvent regulation and television will become an almost unlimited global phenomenon, indistinguishable from Internet multimedia.

The multi-channel Electronic Programme Guide currently presents accessibility problems and these will grow with the size of the offer. Broadcasting is moving much closer to publishing in its legal framework and in the way it 'looks and feels' to end users. Monopoly and cartel television was predictable and therefore an important part of common culture whereas future television content will be increasingly varied and unpredictable. Again, this presents both promise and challenge to VIPs and to librarians.

Telecommunications

It may well be that in spite of the different histories of the computer-mediated Internet and television and radio-mediated broadcasting, the technology that will be at the core of our content experience will be the telephone. Telecommunications has been developing as rapidly as any other medium, moving in 20 years to high-speed cellular delivery that can carry video clips and will soon be able to carry real-time feature-length movies. Combined phone/PDA units allow users full Internet and e-mail access as well as versions of software that make a phone the equivalent of a cable-free computer. For VIPs, the telephone, if it can be made accessible, has a number of key advantages:

- it does not need to be found – rather than searching for a kiosk, the VIP can carry the phone with them;
- it does not need to be learned anew;
- it provides privacy.

This last factor is extremely important. Computer and television access for VIPs is even less private than for their peers. The telephone is by far the best device to access financial, health, sexual and gambling content privately.

Convergence

Computers, televisions and telephones share three components of content access and processing:

- the information controller or input device (remote control, dial, keyboard);
- the processor (television/radio receiver, computer, telephone); and
- the output device (screen, speaker)

These will become separate, cable-free components. Already:

- advanced televisions are split among the wireless remote controller, the screen and the processor;
- the hi-fi has been split among the processor, the wireless controller and the speakers (increasingly wireless);
- the cellular telephone has been split between the screen/processor and wireless earphones;
- computers are split among screens, processors and wireless input devices.

The advent of portable screens and distributed processing power (wireless hot spots etc) will further granularise technological production systems and enable users to assemble their own components or 'borrow' ambient capacity.

The likely outcome of this evolution is that all digital content processing devices will converge into a multi-purpose processor and that this device will be produced in a substantive form for the home and in a microscopic form for portability. These processors will be driven by a highly-personalised input device and data will be produced through a highly-personalised output device. All three will be cable-free.

The implications for VIPs are clear:

- the 'collapse' of a variety of consumer electronics devices (TV, CD, radio, PC etc.) will enable more money to be spent per capita on customised devices;
- accessibility issues will become generic;
- upgrade disadvantages will decrease.

The challenges are equally evident:

- the library system must find a way of meeting the challenge of mediating digital information for VIPs using these highly-personalised devices;
- libraries and governments will have to guard against an increasing digital divide that threatens access for those who cannot afford even the reduced cost of new devices;
- copyright issues must be addressed as platforms converge;
- production standards must be developed that accommodate current and emerging platforms in a rapidly changing environment.

The librarian as facilitator

Before looking at the positive role that librarians can play in the digital information age as content facilitators for VIPs, it is important to set some context. Scarcity of content and the limited capacity to process have often combined seriously to disadvantage VIPs. In the digital age, absolute scarcity is being replaced by comparative disadvantage. While everybody will have access to much more content than at any time in history, the gap between VIPs and their peers will inexorably widen. This will be true even in terms of access to text, and an increasingly multimedia-oriented society with a focus on the visual will further widen the gap.

With respect to the demographic of VIPs, there will always be a small number in need of a high level of academic and professional support between the ages of 15 and 60, but the majority of congenitally blind and visually impaired children will likely continue to have additional disabilities. At the other end of the scale, the massive majority of VIPs will be over the age of 60, increasingly digitally literate but slow to adapt to emerging trends as comfortably as younger people.

Any attempt to keep comparative disadvantage to a minimum means that the 'right to information' librarians routinely champion must be understood in an active way. Not only must the right be practical rather than theoretical, it must be effective. To achieve this, fundamental changes may be required in the understanding of information access channels and how they are used.

Facilitation

Traditionally, the relationship between the librarian and the VIP user has been somewhat 'top-down' and arms-length. This position needs to be replaced by a conscious, collaborative process. Librarians need to understand better the needs of VIPs, but VIPs also need a better understanding of their own needs. In parallel with this, librarians and VIPs need to understand the emerging digital environment better. No matter how difficult this is going to be for librarians, it is going to be much more difficult for VIPs who will have to come to terms in a highly specific way with their own shortcomings. VIPs are in that most problematic of areas – trying to know what it is you do not know. VIPs, particularly blind people, are shielded from a great deal of the world that their peers take for granted, not least the febrile and violent world of much of the media, factual and fictional. This leads to an area where the roles of traditional librarianship are at least contiguous with, and will increasingly overlap with, the roles of teachers, trainers, psychologists and sociologists. For a profession that has gained much of its respect from detachment, this is a serious prospect; but the idea that information is intrinsically rationally estimable and value-free is becoming anachronistic. Yet because the fundamental role of librarianship is facilitation, these problems of boundary can and will be overcome.

Conclusion

There needs to be a realistic assessment of what can and cannot be done about this vibrant, converging world of text and images: not even the Louvre catalogue entry can make the reality of the *Mona Lisa* real to a congenitally blind person. Both the seeing facilitator and the VIP have to accept this. At the other end of the spectrum, there is no reason why seeing people should not be able accurately to describe fixed, physical characteristics such as height, proportionality to other known objects, the ordinary and the curious and, to a degree, colour for those who can still see enough to appreciate it or who can remember what it means. Not many librarians or alternative format producers will have the facility of Proust with Elstir, but a structured approach to constructing a curriculum for visual description is not unimaginable.

Perhaps oddly, then, the whole of the converging digital media environment is surveyed, the ultimate conclusion centres on a human skill, the ability to describe in such a way that the description has an impact on the VIP's understanding of the world in which they live.

Notes

1. See Lockyer et al. (2005).
2. The term 'modified' is used in preference to 'enlarged' for two reasons. First, some VIPs need smaller than standard print. Second, font often is more critical than size.

3

Library services to people who are deaf

Mary Beth Allen

Introduction to deafness

The human hearing mechanism is complex. Defining the deaf community and determining the number of people who belong may be just as complex. The international deaf community is large and extremely diverse, and depending on the context, can include sign language users, bilingual users of sign language and spoken or written language, people with hearing loss who communicate primarily through spoken language and speech reading, adults who have become deaf after acquiring speech, older adults with hearing loss due to age, people who are deaf and use neither sign language or written language, people who are hard of hearing, people who are deaf-blind, family members who can hear, and professionals who serve any of the above (Day and IFLA, 2000: 24) . One or both ears may be affected, and a person's severity of hearing loss can range from 'having a little difficulty understanding conversation' or 'hard of hearing' to complete deafness. Internationally, there is great variation in the way deaf culture is defined.

In wealthier nations, educational mainstreaming has become more common, yet despite this trend, 'a major revival of signing has taken place in the last 40 years that includes international academic support for sign languages and the growing politicisation of Deaf communities worldwide' (Monaghan et al., 2003: 14). Sometimes referred to as the 'invisible disability', hearing loss is not always recognised in libraries.

The incredible sensory privilege we call hearing is measured as intensity of sound, in decibels, on a scale determined by audiologists. Minimal hearing loss is measured at 5–20 decibels; moderate hearing loss is measured at 30–60 decibels; severe hearing loss is measured at 70–90 decibels; profound hearing loss is measured at 90 decibels and above (National Technical Institute for the Deaf, Rochester Institute of Technology, 2006). The two basic types of hearing loss are conductive and sensorineural; it is possible for hearing loss to involve either type or both types simultaneously (Sataloff and Sataloff, 2005: 25–6). While librarians likely will not know what type of hearing loss any individual patron has, by understanding the two types they can help provide the best environment to facilitate learning and information exchange.

Conductive hearing loss is caused by a blockage or barrier to the transmission of sound through the ear's sound-conducting mechanism in the outer or middle ear, resulting in sound being heard in a softened or muffled way. In sensorineural hearing loss, sounds are distorted and speech is not heard clearly.

Demographics and prevalence of hearing loss and deafness

The World Health Organization (WHO) estimated in 2005 that 278 million people worldwide had moderate to profound hearing loss in both ears, and that 80 per cent of those people reside in low and middle-income countries. WHO also reports that the current annual production of hearing aids meets less than 10 per cent of global need, and that in developing countries, fewer than 1 in 40 people who would benefit from a hearing aid have one. Further, WHO indicates that 50 per cent of deafness and hearing loss is avoidable through prevention and early diagnosis (WHO, 2005). In the USA alone, between 20 to 30 million people have some degree of hearing loss, and one million of those are children (National Technical Institute for the Deaf, Rochester Institute of Technology, 2006). According to the Hearing Loss Association of America, this number is expected to double by the year 2030. The prevalence of hearing loss increases with age: as many as one in three people over age 65 have hearing loss. Most hearing losses develop over a period of 25–30 years (Hearing Loss Association of America/Self-Help for Hard of Hearing People, 2006).

Educational and occupational opportunities

Hearing is critical to speech and language development, communication, and learning. For this reason, how and when a person loses their hearing – whether at birth, childhood or adulthood – has a direct impact on how the hearing loss will affect the individual (National Technical Institute for the Deaf, Rochester Institute of Technology, 2006). The age at which hearing loss occurs also has a major impact on what type of intervention can best be used to enable full educational and occupational opportunity.

People who were born deaf, or who became deaf before acquiring significant language skills, may not have received appropriate early intervention and may not have learned to read or produce spoken language that is understandable. For children who are born deaf, the early years of language learning are a critical point because the development of basic communication skills underlies the development of social, psychological and educational foundations later in life. When a child who is deaf has parents who are hearing, making the parents aware of the need for early intervention is crucial so that the child is not isolated. Parents and caregivers must be aware of the importance of learning basic communication skills at an early age, and must have the skills to be able to foster this early learning. 'Most parents of Deaf children have no experience with Deafness, do not know any sign language, and are not aware of what their children are missing' (Rodriguez and Reed, 2003: 38).

Adults who become deaf or hard of hearing later in life may continue to have some residual hearing, and also have the advantage of already having acquired language skills, so they can speak clearly and understand much of the language spoken around them. However, adults who are hard of hearing often are not interested in learning sign language and may not wear hearing aids even when they are available.

The foundation of communication for many people who are deaf or who have significant hearing loss is sign language. Around the globe, unique signed languages are a critical part of deaf communities and incredible variation exists throughout international deaf communities.

Barriers to library service for people who are deaf

Libraries can play a critical role in helping people who are deaf increase and develop literacy skills. However, communication barriers between patrons who are deaf and library staff who are hearing can present a major barrier to library service. Librarians have come to expect that their patrons have acquired basic mainstream literacy skills. But, while large numbers of people who were born deaf are very well educated, their primary language is sign language – a language most library staff members do not know.

Attitudinal barriers can prevent libraries from making the necessary changes to accommodate people who are deaf, whether they are library users or potential employees. As a counterpoint, Sandra Charles, of the University of Dundee, offers a practical account of productive disability awareness training in an academic library setting (Charles, 2005: 453–8).

In the *Australian Library Journal*, Jodi Johnstone makes an analysis of the employment of people with disabilities in libraries and finds attitudinal and technological barriers. Yet she also cites libraries that have used assistive technology to overcome communications barriers, and that have employed very successful deaf librarians and staff (Johnstone 2005, 159–61). Employing a library staff member who is part of the community also can bring significant credibility to the library's programmes.

People who are deaf and reside in rural or undeveloped areas may be poorly served because smaller communities generally offer fewer services. Underdeveloped areas typically have limited Internet access and have less comprehensive provision of medical care, social and educational services. However, in cases where such services are lacking, libraries may fill this void by offering appropriate information services and access to resources, as well as access to a virtual community of peers (Marks, 2005: 7–19). Once barriers to communication and transmission of information are removed, people who are deaf can be more successful in realising their educational and occupational goals.

An excellent example of one library's dedication to overcoming communication barriers can be found in Pinellas County, Florida. There, staff of the Safety Harbor Public Library developed and implemented a literacy programme that reached out to their relatively large population of people who are deaf. The positive result is that people who are deaf now know the library as a place where they can participate and learn effectively, where they can communicate and find the information they need in their daily lives (Rodriguez and Reed, 2003: 38–40).

Examples of excellent library services

The current state of library services to people who are deaf is quite varied.

Australian Karen McQuigg writes that in countries where legislation has required public institutions to provide equal access and opportunity for people with disabilities, progress has been made, especially where an explicit action plan is outlined and mandated. However, McQuigg notes, 'non-compliance with the spirit of disability legislation may be happening because many librarians think compliance primarily means physical access to the building, rather than what happens inside' (McQuigg, 2003: 373). McQuigg makes the point that, 'Not only are the deaf not on the agendas of public libraries but anecdotal evidence suggests that the situation is mutual' (McQuigg, 2003: 368). This implies that libraries may need to be proactive to reach out to the deaf community. That said, public libraries have generally taken the lead in service provision, perhaps because they are more involved in community outreach activity.

The comprehensive library service programme described by Rosa Rodriguez and Monica Reed in *Public Libraries* offers many examples of effective services developed in response to the needs of the deaf community in Pinellas County, Florida. The library partnered with other agencies within the community, including the St. Petersburg College interpreter training programme, a neighbourhood family centre, a women's club, and church-based organisations. They received grant funding to build a literacy programme. They built a collection of library materials of interest to people who are deaf, including print material and videos on deaf culture and American Sign Language. The library started sign language classes, and was amazed at the huge turnout of children and adults. The programme has continued to grow and the library has become involved in a wide range of community-based learning activities and social events (Rodriguez and Reed, 2003: 38–41).

In the UK, the Gateshead Public Library offers accessible information sources through its Access to Information and Reading Services programme. Included is a deaf resources section, as well as a group of services for people who are blind or partially sighted (Hannah, 2003: 50–2). At the University of Padua, library staff report that current legislation has increased the impetus for a 'new culture of disability', where the key is providing equal access to information. They stress the importance of training library staff to understand better the needs of people with motor, visual and hearing disabilities (De Gasperi and Callegari, 2003: 463–71).

In a recent *IFLA Journal*, Margaret E. S. Forrest describes her experience at the Fife Library at the University of Dundee (Forrest, 2006: 13–17). There, IFLA's 2005 *Checklist: Access to Libraries for Persons with Disabilities* was used to identify and help overcome barriers to the provision of good service. Forrest also explains how disability legislation in the UK has provided important incentive for libraries to improve their services (Forrest, 2006: 13).

The San Francisco Public Library has developed a Deaf Services Center at its main library, with a full complement of resources for both children and adults. Examples of services offered include Sorenson Video Relay Service, which enables video relay calls through a certified ASL interpreter; information on programmes, classes on sign language, deaf studies, interpreting and other topics of interest; assistive listening devices; meeting rooms outfitted with listening systems; video/DVD viewing on televisions equipped with closed-caption decoders; public text telephones (TTYs) and amplified telephones; and exhibits of work by deaf artists. The Library has also produced a four-part video series called, 'American Culture: The Deaf Perspective,' available on their website (*http://sfpl.lib.ca.us/librarylocations/accessservices/deafservices.htm*).

School librarians also have employed successful techniques to encourage children who are deaf or who have hearing loss develop their reading skills. Linda Lajoie reports in *School Library Journal* that simply including children who are deaf in literacy activities such as story hours has a positive effect. 'By seeing a librarian read aloud, deaf children learn to enjoy and value books. Kids who are deaf can share stories and gain knowledge if they're included in this activity' (Lajoie, 2003: 43). Lajoie also used basic sign language materials to illustrate stories, and partnered with other librarians and a school for children who are deaf to engage children in reading activities and bridge the literacy gap with their hearing peers (Lajoie, 2003: 43).

Among academic institutions, Gallaudet University is an international leader for its research on the history, language and culture of people who are deaf. In an article in *Education Libraries*, Thomas Harrington (1998: 3–12) described the richness of the collection. Both the Gallaudet University Library and the Laurent Clerc National Deaf Education Center at Gallaudet are world-renowned centres for information on all aspects of deafness and related areas. They maintain comprehensive websites to share this information.

With more than 1,000 students who are deaf or have hearing loss, Rochester Institute of Technology Libraries also promotes excellent services for students and academics who are deaf. At their public service desks, they use a program called Interpretype to facilitate communication between signers and non-signers. They offer TTYs, a captioned and ASL video collection, webcams and an Internet relay service, and they offer headphones and a Wacom writing tablet to library users (see *http://library .rit.edu/*).

Ideas to improve library service

Keeping students and library patrons on track, 'even at places like NTID and Gallaudet University in Washington, DC, one of [America's] premier institutions of higher learning explicitly founded and designed for deaf and hard-of-hearing students – takes devotion and persistence on the part of students, teachers, and employers' (Amato, 2006: 53). The same can be said for libraries.

Fortunately, librarians seeking to improve their services have access to the work of their peers. The basis for much current work was a 1991 International Federation of Library Associations and Institutions (IFLA) publication, which is now available in a second edition. Edited by John Michael Day, former University Librarian at Gallaudet University Library, *Guidelines for Library Services to Deaf*

People covers major issues related to library personnel, communication, building appropriate collections, developing services, and marketing programmes for people who are deaf (Day and IFLA, 2000: 1–25). In 1996, the Association of Specialized and Cooperative Library Agencies (ASCLA) of the American Library Association (ALA) published a version of this document, adapted specifically for libraries in the USA, entitled *Guidelines for Library and Information Services for the American Deaf Community* (Goddard, 1996: 1–20).

In the 2001 ASCLA publication, *Planning for Library Services to People with Disabilities* (Rubin and ASCLA, 2001: 75), a tip sheet is included for communicating with patrons who are deaf or hard of hearing. Specific communication tips include:

- 'Approach the patron so you can be seen.

- Get the patron's attention before you start speaking.

- Ask the patron how s/he prefers to communicate and then accommodate the request. Do not assume a knowledge of sign language. Do not leave to find a person who can sign unless the patron requests it.

- Reduce background noise or move to a quieter location.

- Always face the patron as you speak and maintain eye contact.

- If you are using an interpreter, be sure to speak directly to the patron, not to the interpreter.

- Speak at a normal pace, enunciating carefully; do not exaggerate your lip movements or mumble as this makes speechreading difficult.

- Keep your mouth visible – do not obscure it with your hands or by chewing gum or food.

- Be aware of lighting. For example, do not stand in front of a light source because that makes it difficult to speechread or to pick up visual cues.

- If a hard of hearing patron has hearing aids or other assistive listening devices, give her/him an opportunity to adjust the equipment.

- If the patron does not seem to understand you, write it down.'

Leila Monaghan and her co-authors provide a global overview in *Many Ways to be Deaf: International Variation in Deaf Communities*. This fascinating book describes how complex, new signed languages continue to be invented in places where people who are deaf are isolated from other signing groups. Contributed chapters address the diverse deaf cultures and languages in Austria, Brazil, Britain, Ireland, Japan, Nicaragua, Nigeria, Russia, South Africa, Switzerland, Taiwan, Thailand, the USA and Vietnam (Monaghan et al., 2003).

A successful programme of services for the deaf community in Cleveland, Ohio is described by Abigail Noland in *Public Libraries*. Noland stresses the importance of the library director's commitment and the vision and energy of the entire staff to maintaining and expanding services, even with dwindling resources (Noland, 2003: 20–1).

A practical example of providing inclusive library and information services in the UK can be found in *Health Information and Libraries Journal*. In her article, Sarah Playforth advances the 'social model approach' in which library staff simply ask the patron 'what do you need?' in order to develop fully inclusive services (Playforth, 2004: 54).

Another excellent source of information on providing library services to people who are deaf is the Friends of

Libraries for Deaf Action (FOLDA) 'Red Notebook,' originated in 1979 by deaf librarian and advocate Alice L. Hagemeyer. The Red Notebook is geared to US libraries, but much of its advice applies to a global audience. As of autumn 2006, a revision is in process, which will be available on FOLDA's website (*www.folda.net*).

For assistance with building library collections that provide information on deafness, hearing loss and deaf culture, as well as materials targeted for use by people who are deaf, Gallaudet University Library devotes a section of its website (*http://library.gallaudet.edu*) to 'deaf-related resources'. For additional suggestions on how to choose material on deafness and sign language, a practical article called 'Hands-on collection building,' by Kathleen MacMillan appeared in *School Library Journal* (MacMillan, 2004: 46–7).

Implementing technological solutions

Technological solutions already offer a bridge for people who are deaf or who have hearing loss, and further development will continue to enhance communication paths. The most common assistive device for people who are deaf or who have hearing loss is the hearing aid, which amplifies sound while simultaneously reducing background noise. Another device is the FM system, which allows the speaker to wear a transmitting microphone, while the listener wears a small receiver with volume control that is usually attached to earphones. Sound field systems are FM wireless public address systems that amplify the speaker's voice through speakers that are strategically located through the room. Other assistive devices include forms of listening and alerting technology such as telephone and cell phone amplifiers, doorbell flashing signals, vibratory wristwatches, and television listeners. State-of-the-art TTYs for international use are very quick and fairly accurate. The same idea is used in e-mail, chat and instant text messaging. Tom Peters and Lori Bell have written a good overview of new technologies that libraries can use to improve their accessibility for people who are deaf. They encourage librarians to jump into instant messaging as a low-cost first step (Peters and Bell, 2006: 18–21).

Text telephones/pagers transmit and receive typewritten messages via telecommunication lines. Standard text messaging can reach most people who use cellular phones. Another access option is automatic speech recognition technology that recognises and converts the spoken word into text so it can be read. New communicative practices have developed that use visual language to allow communication via webcam and video chat. An interesting study on the incorporation of webcam technology into the communicative practices of the deaf community was reported by Elizabeth Keating and Gene Mirus in *Language in Society*. Their article describes experiments incorporating a variety of communication forms, such as sign language, TTY, text messaging, computer-mediated videophone and e-mail. It encourages people to adapt their communication styles to the needs of specific audiences (Keating and Mirus, 2003: 693–714).

Captioning of spoken information can be done 'on the fly' at meetings or presentations by a captionist in the audience and also is incorporated into many movies and television media. It is particularly suited to large group presentations. A form of captioning, C-Print, is a computer-based speech to print transcription system developed at the National

Technical Institute for the Deaf (NTID), at the Rochester Institute of Technology and used in many schools as a communication device for students who are deaf or hard of hearing. Other advanced products use speech-recognition technology to translate speech into text and sign language that can be projected onto a screen for audience members to see.

There are also a number of electronic tools that can link sign with other languages. One such development, called MySignLink, is hailed as, 'the kind of innovation that may very well revolutionise the way deaf children acquire vocabulary and learn to read' (McCaffrey, 2004: 48–9). Similar initiatives exist for other sign languages. For example, French sign language users can consult *LSF sur le Web* (*http://ufr6.univ-paris8.fr/desshandi/supl/projets/site_lsf/*), a site by students of Paris University, which contains videos of many individual signs. Sign On-Line (*http://www.signonline.org.uk*) is a successful joint project of several university and community partners in the UK to provide expert online training and distance education for tutors of British Sign Language.

With increased emphasis on wireless technologies, libraries using portable wireless applications must ensure these tools are accessible to people with disabilities. Accessibility options such as using visual cues along with or instead of audible ones already are in place in most major software products and are extremely useful. New speech recognition tools developed by major software companies offer real-time transcription, display, editing, annotation and presentation of spoken information such as lectures and webcasts. Multi-modal features make such tools appropriate in a broad array of learning environments. Flexible output options make access easy for people who are deaf or hard of hearing, as well as for people who are blind or who are learning a language. Searchable access to text archives is beneficial to everyone (IBM, 2006).

To be most effective, accessible technology should be customisable by the user; should offer content via multiple modes (moving images, text, graphics, music and audio) controlled by the user; and should work with a variety of user interfaces. The ultimate goal of such design is flexibility, so that any number of diverse users can manipulate elements of the content to suit their unique needs (Carey, 2005). As always, the real challenge will be putting the technology into the hands of those who need it.

Using the Internet to improve service

> The World Wide Web is particularly suited as a communication medium for the deaf community. A wealth of deaf-related online information is available on subject specific, special purpose, and comprehensive sites that provide important resources for deaf people, their families, and involved professionals. (Day, 1999: 5).

Libraries can help improve web usefulness by teaching search strategies and critical evaluation techniques. Day goes on to note that as a source of information, a graphic interface and an effective medium of visual communication, the Internet is particularly beneficial to people who are deaf. 'The combination of those two aspects, graphic interface and effective medium of visual communication, has led to a particularly rich body of deaf-related information available on the Web' (Day, 1999: 6).

Internet resources

The following list provides web addresses for sources of information and organisations providing information on and services to people who are deaf or have hearing loss.

- Alexander Graham Bell Association for the Deaf and Hard of Hearing (*www.agbell.org*): With chapters in the USA and a network of international affiliates, this support organisation offers advocacy, financial aid, programmes and events for people with hearing loss. Publishes the periodicals *Volta Voices* and *The Volta Review*; the site also offers a bookstore.

- American Academy of Audiology (*www.audiology.org*): A professional organisation of, by, and for audiologists. The site includes consumer quicklinks and a directory of audiologists, searchable by city and state.

- American Deafness and Rehabilitation Association (*www.adara.org*): A professional association that seeks to improve the lives of deaf persons. Publishes *JADARA: The Journal for Professionals Networking for Excellence in Service Delivery with Individuals who are Deaf and Hard of Hearing.*

- American Speech Language Hearing Association (*www.asha.org*): This professional, scientific and credentialing association offers extensive information to the public, as well as to students and professional members about speech, language and hearing disorders.

- Canadian Hearing Society (*www.chs.ca*): A comprehensive group that provides information and services that enhance the independence of people who are deaf or hard of hearing, and that encourages prevention of hearing loss.

- Children of Deaf Adults International (*www.coda-international.org*): A nonprofit organisation for the adult hearing children of deaf parents that promotes family awareness and growth and offers regional retreats and an international conference for members.

- Deafness Research Foundation (*www.drf.org*): A source of private funding for basic and clinical research in hearing science.

- Deafsign (*www.deafsign.com*): This British site provides information, contacts, and discussion on deafness and sign language.

- Friends of Libraries for Deaf Action/The Red Notebook (*www.folda.net*).

- Hearing International (*www.hearinginter.com*): Works with the World Health Organization, the International Federation of Otorhinolaryngological Societies, and the International Society of Audiology to support research aimed at preventing hearing impairment..

- *IFLA Checklist: Access to Libraries for Persons with Disabilities* (*www.ifla.org/VII/s9/nd1/iflapr-89e.pdf*): This 2005 document is also written by the IFLA section below.

- IFLA Libraries Serving Disadvantaged Persons Section (*www.ifla.org/VII/s9/index.htm*): This International Federation of Library Associations and Institutions section includes services to people who are deaf. Includes the 2000 document *Guidelines to Library Services to Deaf People*.

- International Deaf Children's Society (*www.idcs.info*): The Society seeks to empower families with clear information and support. The site offers a global directory of deaf organisations.

- International Hearing Society (*www.ihsinfo.org*): A worldwide association of hearing healthcare professionals, IHS advocates for advanced education, training and competence for its members. The site also provides consumer health information.

- Laurent Clerc National Deaf Education Center (*http://clerccenter.gallaudet.edu/*): The Clerc Center's mission is to help US children who are deaf or hard of hearing by offering information, supporting service projects and training opportunities. The Center operates an elementary school and a secondary school as model schools for the deaf.

- Michigan State University's American Sign Language Browser (*http://commtechlab.msu.edu/products/asl/index .html*): Offers a CD-ROM ASL Browser for sale at $19.99. The Browser contains over 2,500 signs with over 4,500 English synonyms.

- National Institute on Deafness and Other Communication Disorders (*www.nidcd.nih.gov*): Supports and conducts research on communication disorders. Provides information in Spanish, as well as in English, on a variety of communication disorders.

- National Technical Institute for the Deaf (NTID)/ Rochester Institute of Technology (*www.ntidweb.rit.edu*): An international model for educating and preparing deaf and hard of hearing students for technology-related careers, NTID offers associate, bachelor's and master's degrees.

- Royal National Institute for Deaf People (*www.rnid .org.uk*): Provides services and training, supports research and campaigns to make daily life better for people with deafness or hearing loss. Offers comprehensive information and fact sheets on all aspects of hearing loss, prevention and treatment, as well as British Sign Language.

- Self Help for Hard of Hearing People/Hearing Loss Association of America (*www.shhh.org*): Aims to open communication to people with hearing loss by providing information, education, support and advocacy. The site offers a bookstore. The former Cochlear Implant Association is in process of becoming a section of this association.

- Sign Languages of the World, by Country (*http://library .gallaudet.edu/dr/deaffaqs.html*) – prepared by Tom Harrington, Gallaudet University Library.

- World Federation of the Deaf (*www.wfdeaf.org*): An international organisation that represents deaf people worldwide. Works closely with the United Nations to promote human rights of deaf people, especially in developing countries.

4

Adaptive technology for people with physical disabilities using information and communications technology

C. M. Tilley, C. S. Bruce and G. Hallam

Introduction

Whether serving academic, public or special populations, libraries are charged with making information available to their constituents. Electronic access, networked resources and other forms of information and communications technology (ICT) are becoming the norm for information delivery. Technology, largely a boon to people with disabilities, may be difficult for some people to access. Assistive technology bridges this gap by providing innovative ways to help people access ICT. By using appropriate assistive technology, libraries can improve information access – and quality of life – for large numbers of their patrons.

This chapter explores assistive technology and its implications for people who have disabilities. Using the Australian experience as a foundation, the authors discuss assistive technology and disability; how assistive technology facilitates ICT use; how libraries can promote assistive technology; and how libraries can select assistive technology that will be used by their patrons.

Rob Garrett, the Assistive Technology Project Group Leader, Research & Development, Engineering and Support Team, NovitaTech (*http://www.novitatech.org.au/*), South Australia, has proposed a partnership for the research and development of technologies that will positively affect the health, wellbeing and independent living of the elderly and people living with a disability. The partnership emphasises habilitation, as well as rehabilitation, aging in place, and prevention of injury and disability. Within the telecommunications area, proposed activities are:

- to identify and understand the needs and wants of people who cannot use a traditional telecommunications product or service;

- to research ways and methods to provide accessible telecommunications products and services;

- to work in partnership with the telecommunications industry to develop appropriate products and services that are accessible for all people.

Adaptive technology and disability

Adaptive technology (also called *assistive technology*)[1] refers to products that help people who cannot use regular versions of products – primarily people with disabilities affecting their ability to walk or use their arms. According to the US Assistive Technology Act 1998, assistive technology refers to any 'product, device, or equipment, whether acquired commercially, modified or customised, that is used to maintain, increase, or improve the functional capabilities of individuals with disabilities'. The term 'assistive technology' is used to refer to 'a broad range of devices, services, strategies and practices that are applied to ameliorate the problems faced by individuals who have disabilities' (Baum, 1998; Cook and Hussey, 1995; Lupton and Seymore, 2000). Common computer-related assistive technology products[2] for people with physical disabilities include screen magnifiers, large-key keyboards, alternative input devices such as touch screen displays, over-sized trackballs and joysticks, speech recognition programs and text readers (Brooks, 1991).

Since the 1970s, the understanding of disability has changed dramatically. Once perceived as a largely medical problem affecting only a small number of people, it is now regarded as a major social and political issue. The most common types of disability are caused by physical impairments,[3] for example, 2.6 million people or 14 per cent of Australians are thus affected (ABS, 2000). The Australian Bureau of Statistics 2003 survey on aging, disability and carers indicated that the disability rate remained substantially unchanged since 1996 with one in five people, or 20 per cent of Australians, reporting a disability. One in ten people in Australia identified that they used equipment, or an aid, to help them cope with their condition or manage everyday life. The disability rate steadily increased with age from 4 per cent of 0–4 year olds, to 41 per cent of 65–69 year olds, to 92 per cent of people aged 90 years or older. The proportion of people who stated that they needed help with self-care, mobility and/or communication activities remained stable at 6.3 per cent of the population (ABS, 2004).

Traditionally, people with disabilities were defined as 'disabled' because of their specific impairments, such as loss of physical function as the result of illness or injury. More recently the International Classification System of Impairments, Activities and Participation has proposed a social model of disability that views disability as an inability to participate in activities (WHO, 1997). Consequently, the focus has shifted from the inadequacies of the individual with an impairment to the activity restriction or barriers in society that exclude people from participation. This has resulted in a number of legislative initiatives being enacted to assist people with disabilities to enter the workforce and access the technology they require to carry out various tasks.

Adaptive technology enables people with physical disabilities to access ICT

In Australian society today, people with disabilities are increasingly demanding equal access to the full range of community resources, information and opportunities. Disability per se is no longer accepted as being a barrier to gaining an education, taking part in civil and political life, enjoying a fulfilling social life, raising a family, being involved in the community, or engaging in paid and unpaid work. On the contrary, the community now actively supports the participation of people with disabilities. Businesses and community organisations are expected to make reasonable efforts to make sure that people with disabilities can use their goods and services. Governments too are expected to facilitate the participation and inclusion of people with disabilities and are rightly held to a higher level of accountability by the community in this regard (ABS, 1996, 1999; AIHW, 2000).

Over the years, consumer advocates have identified and promoted five other consumer responsibilities: solidarity, critical awareness, action, social concern and environmental awareness. These various rights impact on adaptive technology and how it empowers and enables people with physical disabilities to access ICT.

It is common knowledge that persons with disabilities benefit from access to, and use of, ICT (Vincent and Morin, 1999). However, people with physical disabilities have a harder time using technology when it is physically difficult to use a computer (Covington, 1998; Cowan and Turner-Smith, 1999; Seiler et al., 1997). Modifications to standard computer equipment and/or the use of modified techniques, including individualised set-up and positioning, help overcome some difficulties experienced by persons with disabilities and are regarded as the first point of intervention. Sometimes, simple strategies, such as altering the position or height of the keyboard and/or the mouse, are all that is required to enable the person to use a computer more efficiently. Some people with disabilities require the use of specialised equipment as well. The best equipment for them to use is decided by the provision of information and advice on a range of possible equipment options and, wherever possible, an individualised trial of the equipment. Of course, simple strategies of use also are teamed with non-standard or specialised equipment options for people with disabilities.

Computer access options refer to a range of strategies and equipment that are useful in assisting people with the difficulties encountered in using a computer. These options include alternative seating, positioning, keyboard, mouse and software options. Environmental control technology refers to equipment that enables a person to control their environment when their ability to use standard methods of control has been lost or diminished. For example, specialised remote control devices that are used in place of a number of standard remote controls and also incorporate the on and off control of lighting and electrical appliances. Switch access provides a means of accessing a range of activities including communication, computer access, leisure and environmental control. They are useful for people whose functional movement severely limits their ability to participate independently in a range of activities – an individualised switch set-up enables them to have some independence. Switch access is used with activities such as listening to music, operating a computer or operating a communication device.

There is a wide variety of switches available, with the most appropriate choice dependent on a person's particular needs and skills. Some switches can be pressed down, others only need to be touched and some only need the person to move close to them. Switches may be placed in any position and used with any body movement. Some specialised switches can be operated by puffs and sips of air or by electrical activity within the muscles.

Keyboard options include keyboards with enlarged key areas, reduced-size keyboards, programmable keyboards, ergonomic keyboards and on-screen keyboards. Keyboard accessories are available for both standard and alternative keyboards. These can be as simple as stickers that enhance the visual clarity of keyboard displays or key-guards, helping people accurately target keys. There are also mouse options for people with disabilities who have difficulty using a standard mouse. Alternative options include trackballs, trackpads, joysticks and remote sensor units. Software is available that assists with specific mouse functions. Switch-operated scanning mouse software is also available.

If a person with disabilities is unable to use any keyboard options, speech recognition software may be a suitable option, but the learning curve and editing required can make it unattractive in a library setting. Speech recognition software recognises the words spoken by a person and translates them into text or commands for the computer to carry out. As this software is quite complex, it must be considered carefully for suitability and back-up options (for example, an on-screen keyboard). Current versions have improved significantly with regards to both the training and operation of the software. Desktop USB microphones are also available and are useful for people who are unable to position the standard headset microphone independently.

An environmental control unit or device (ECU) provides an alternative means of operating various appliances within an environment. In a library, an ECU might control appliances (e.g. television, VCR); turn on/off lights; or facilitate telephone use. Appropriate selection of such equipment can enable people with disabilities to be more independent. It is important to ensure the right match between the person and the technology. The questions to ask when investigating environmental control options in the library include the following:

- What library equipment requires an alternative control device?

- What environment(s) will the device be used in?

- What movement(s) can be used to control or access the device within these environments?

- What type of display interface is required?

- How easy is it for patrons to learn to use the device?

- What are the set-up and training needs?

- Are funds available to cover purchase, installation, maintenance and training costs?

The most appropriate equipment choice to meet individual needs is best decided by the provision of information and advice on a range of possible equipment options in relation to the factors above. Wherever possible, individualised trial of equipment is also recommended. Over the past few years, there has been a significant growth in the range of equipment available and this has greatly enhanced the possibilities for people who are unable to use the standard methods of environmental control.

Central to any computer access solution is also the positioning of both person and equipment. Each individual person with a disability requires a unique mix of techniques and/or equipment that enable them to be successful at using their computer. For example, if a person with disabilities has difficulty in using standard computer software programs, there is a range of specialised software that caters to a variety of needs and skills. Examples include word processing software that speaks out what is typed and word processing software that displays text and symbols. There is also access enhancement software that predicts or completes text to reduce keystrokes required. This increases typing efficiency and improves the user's endurance. Specialised software helps people who are switch users or who have literacy or numeracy difficulties.

The assistive technology information centre model

In Australia, a model has emerged to provide unbiased information about assistive technology via the assistive technology information centre. An assistive technology information centre is a non-profit, non-government community organisation.[4] These centres do not sell any equipment, nor are they aligned with only the one equipment range or supplier – all suppliers are invited to display their relevant equipment. This service has a comprehensive, state-of-the-art range of assistive technology equipment including alternative computer input devices, voice output communication devices, accessible hardware and software, electronic and wireless environmental control systems, switches, switch-operated equipment and positioning equipment necessary to support the effective use of this equipment. Both speech pathologists and occupational therapists staff the assistive technology information centre. They provide professional, impartial advice, consultation and education about assistive technology options. This consultation and information service enables people with disabilities, and those who support them, to trial a range of equipment options, customised to their individual needs and goals. Consequently, they are able to make an informed decision about the assistive technology equipment options that best meet their individual needs, goals and physical limitations. Furthermore, the assistive technology information centre has a referral process that is open to anyone wanting to explore assistive technology options, including people with a disability, their family members, carers or their service providers.

Information services operating where such centres exist help patrons by providing referrals and promoting awareness of the centres. Larger North American public libraries routinely have technology centres and sometimes even loan equipment to their clients to trial in their own homes. While other countries would undoubtedly like to enjoy similar arrangements, in Australia, it is the state and university libraries that provide some assistive technology equipment on site to enable people with disabilities to access their resources and services.

Including patrons in assistive technology selection

Despite the assistance and promise of independence offered by many devices and the growth in assistive technology options, the rate of assistive technology non-use and abandonment, and discontinuance remains high – on average about one-third of all devices provided to consumers (Hocking, 1999). According to the study's interviews, the single most important reason why devices are not used by consumers is a lack of consumer involvement in their selection (Scherer, 2000). If the device meets the person's performance expectations and is easy and comfortable to use, then a good match of person and technology has been achieved. The perspective of the user must increasingly be the driving force in device selection, not the affordability of the equipment and the speed with which it is obtained. To reduce device discontinuance, non-use, and abandonment, increasing attention needs to be paid to the person with a disability as a unique user of a particular device. Assistive technology users differ as much personally as they do functionally. Functionality in use of technology is evident in all the interviews. Each potential user brings to the assistive technology evaluation and selection process a unique set of needs and expectations, as well as readiness for use. To achieve better assistive technology outcomes, these factors are ideally assessed so that the assistive technology can be customised to the user, training and trial use of devices arranged and additional supports identified.

The impact of assistive technology and ICT on people with disabilities

Information literacy skills are fundamental to the successful use of ICT and information services for people with physical disabilities. Information literacy can contribute to participative citizenship; social inclusion; acquisition of skills; innovation and enterprise; the creation of new knowledge; personal, vocational, corporate and organisational empowerment; and learning for life (ALIA, 2003). While this definition of information literacy affords an insight into the notions encompassed by the term, a foremost scholar argues that there are seven 'faces' of information literacy worth embracing (Bruce, 1997: 154).

Library and information services professionals have chosen to undertake a responsibility to develop the information literacy of their clients. They support governments at all levels, and the corporate, community, professional, educational and trade union sectors, in promoting and facilitating the development of information literacy for all as a high priority. In Australia, the Council of Australian University Librarians (CAUL) adopted the Australian School Library Association (ASLA) Statement on Information Literacy in 1994. The Australian Library and Information Association (ALIA) adopted their policy statement on information literacy for all Australians in 2001 and amended it in 2003 (ALIA, 2003).

Information literacy promotes the free flow of information and ideas vital to a thriving culture, economy and democracy. ALIA believes that a thriving national and global culture, economy and democracy will be advanced best by persons who recognise their information need. They also need to be able to identify, locate, access, evaluate and apply that information and to be information and technologically literate as deemed desirable per the 'Thematic Debate on Information Literacy' (UNESCO, 2005a).

Information pertaining to the availability and applicability of assistive technology is a case in point. Some of the recent technological developments have changed the methods of ICT access in the context of the emerging 'information society'. The ACTS AVANTI ACO42 project 'Adaptive and Adaptable Interactions for Multimedia Telecommunications Applications' (1995–98) aimed to enable the integration of people with disabilities into this emerging information environment, with the main focus relating to the access of information. The ACTS AVANTI ACO42 project was based on the universal design approach and on the concepts of adaptability and adaptivity of information contents and user-to-terminal interfaces, building on the results of other related research and development activities in Europe. The field trials tested applications dealing with access to information related to the accessibility of sites of interest or importance for the autonomous mobility of people with disabilities (for example, transportation, hotels, public buildings and so on). The information was integrated into general databases for tourists and presented when requested by the user (Emiliani, 1997; Stephanidis and Emiliani, 1999). Fortuitously, these same databases are available in public and special libraries.[5]

People who previously had very little autonomy now use computers to speak, write, read, study, manage finances, organise their own lives, express themselves creatively, develop skills and hobbies, and gain employment. This has been an unequalled historic opportunity for people with disabilities to become more independent and productive. Furthermore, the future of virtual reality, robotics, videoconferencing, mind switches and so on continues to unfold. However, there are no coherent government policies on assistive technology and there seems to be no bureaucratic understanding of the economic necessity for such technology (Galvin, 1997). For example, it does not even feature in the Australian Commonwealth State Disability Agreement, which allocates key policy responsibilities on disability matters between the Commonwealth and State governments.

The importance of enabling legislation

Legislation in the USA, Sweden, Denmark and other countries has greatly improved the availability of assistive technology by requiring equivalent access for people who have disabilities. In other countries, however, legislative progress has not been so swift.

Australia represents a good example of the work that still needs to be done. Smith (2003), so commendable for his work in Australia, has pointed out the country's monumental policy failure in the area of assistive technology. There are at least four different Commonwealth Departments mandated to cover assistive technology issues (with responsibility for areas such as health, human services, employment, education and training), but none in fact have done so. There are various Australian State Departments that also cover assistive technology issues, but only Health Departments flirt with the issue, through the minimal and chaotic 'Program of Appliances for Disabled People' schemes.

Smith accuses Australia of having nothing remotely comparable with the US Assistive Technology Act 1998. He argues that what is needed are creative government policies in Australia to fund, research and test assistive technology, and widely available opportunities to trial and evaluate this technology. His suggestions include taking assistive technology directly to people who live in rural and remote regions (in fact, Queensland's Independent Living Centre (ILC) provides regular regional tours); technical support services for employers and job agencies; training for those who give advice and for end-users; publicised case studies of successes; and funding for the equipment itself. Many of these activities can be advertised and coordinated through local libraries.

Smith asserts that above all, channels of effective communication are needed to get useable information (in multimedia formats) out to therapists, teachers, job placement agencies, disability workers, employers and people with disabilities. Smith declares the widespread use of assistive technology by people with disabilities is an economic issue, in that the appropriate policies will increase the employment and employability of people with disabilities, save the government welfare money, and enrich the lives of people with disabilities. It then becomes a win-win situation and overwhelming good sense (Smith, 2003: 20). Again, libraries, in their role as community information providers, can be leaders in such communications efforts.

In their research into telecommunications options for people with physical disabilities, Nguyen et al. (2004) have also noted the assistive technology deficit. They present it as an ongoing challenge. Their research trialled and evaluated new configurable 'off-the-shelf' technological options that improve many lifestyle aspects for people with physical disabilities. They considered alternative solutions to improve the awareness and the telecommunications and ICT experiences of people with physical disabilities. Their research aimed to enable these members of the community to participate and experience telecommunications technology to the same extent as able-bodied people currently do. These researchers concluded that with the right policies, processes and support in place, current off-the-shelf solutions have helped to alleviate problems and improve the lifestyle, social interaction, security and independence of many people with physical disabilities.

It is desirable that similar legislation, such as the North American Assistive Technology Act 2004, be introduced into all countries that do not have it, as soon as possible, and furthermore, that an independent, disability equipment programme be instituted. The current situation for obtaining assistive telecommunications equipment in Australia is inadequate. Customers with disabilities who need assistive equipment are not able to take advantage of competition in the marketplace. The situation is anti-competitive and discriminates against people with disabilities, limits their choice of carrier and the type of service. In the competitive telecommunications marketplace, a radical re-think is needed to make sure that consumers with disabilities are not discriminated against in taking up competitive deals because of their lack of access to a disability equipment programme. Urgent action needs to be taken by the Australian Commonwealth Government and the Australian Communications Industry (ACI) to investigate ways of operating a comprehensive, independent, centralised, consumer involved and universally available disability equipment programme. At last, government action seems likely.[6]

Removing barriers to library ICT access

Even with legislation in place and assistive technology selected, there are four major types of barrier to people with disabilities in using ICT and thereby accessing information.

These are costs/affordability, physical barriers associated with lack of training, technological problems related to connectivity, and social barriers. Costs are a barrier, because most people with disabilities have limited economic resources (Williamson et al., 2000: 9). Other barriers for persons with disabilities being able to use ICT may also include being on the wrong side of a digital divide, being information illiterate and technologically illiterate. Barriers may also include connection problems for rural and remote people, the isolation of the double-edged sword controversy[7] and the inaccessibility of chat rooms to people with physical disabilities. Also identified as barriers are a lack of information or inadequate support in the person's environment to set up equipment.

Some of the cost barriers identified include the set-up costs for the hardware and software (for example, voice recognition), assistive technology, the Internet service provider (ISP) and the ongoing telecommunication cost, or broadband. Solutions to this include cheap recycled 'green' computers, or computers available from local councils according to income/assets testing or, in Australia, from Technical Aid to the Disabled. For example, in 2005, Technical Aid to the Disabled and the Internet service provider ISPOne formed a partnership committed to providing Internet access to people receiving the Disability Support Pension.[8] Reduced earning capacity and the constant changes in technology exacerbate the problem of cost barriers. Technology changes approximately every two years and any government-assisted funding system is not geared to such a short turn-around time.

Another example of the kind of frustration professionals experience is the fact that high-level disability needs attract similar financial support to low-level needs. These problems mean that the 'disability dollar' is often dissipated. As outlined above, little is understood of the needs of assistive technology users and the quality of the outcomes achieved. Furthermore, while the Technology-Related Assistance for Individuals with Disabilities Act 1988 (PL 100–407) was introduced in the USA to create new funding systems for technology assistance (Galvin, 1997), there is no legislation relating specifically to the provision of assistive technology in many other western countries. Consequently, assistive technology resources/services are frequently fragmented and poorly funded with uncertain futures (Smith, 2003). Libraries can help by providing free, unbiased access to mainstream computer services and assistive technology, but this may be of limited value to people who are unable to travel to the library facility.

Lack of training for people with disabilities in using the technology is another major barrier. Pell's 1999 study quantified the extent to which the two types of technology, computers and assistive devices, were being used by people with physical disabilities in Australia. Additionally, the amount and types of computer education and training being undertaken by people with physical disabilities were also examined. The particular target group was chosen because the existing literature suggested that the technology helped its members overcome many of the mobility and access problems which are often the only barriers preventing them from obtaining greater levels of independence (Pell et al., 1999: 56). The study found that comparison between present computer ability and demographic variables indicated that there are significant relationships between the level of computer ability and the age of the respondent, the age of disability onset, and the type of disability. Respondents with quadriplegia were more likely to have higher levels of present computer ability than did those persons with paraplegia. The findings also indicated that training was required in two main areas. The first was in the basic use of computers and standard productivity tools, followed by more advanced skills. Such abilities would be highly sought in a society dominated by information production, transfer and analysis, and would improve employment prospects for people with disabilities. The second area for training was in the use of assistive devices (Andrich, 1999; Pell et al., 1999: 58–9). In 2006, this position is unfortunately still relevant and needs to be addressed. In a library setting, the problem is compounded, as both staff and patrons must be trained.

Connectivity also is an ongoing issue. Ironically, new products are readily available in the information technology area and part of a highly competitive market. For assistive technology to connect to and work with rapidly changing new technology is always a challenge. This is where national, regional and international standards become important. Considerable work is being done to develop and meet accessibility standards so that future technology standards do not disenfranchise people with disabilities. At present, however, libraries may have to take a 'best guess' approach when selecting assistive technology where standards conflict. A good approach is to network with affiliated and neighbouring libraries and institutions to promote a consistent approach.

Universal design, design for all, or inclusive design is a very important concept for ensuring that mainstream manufacturers produce, into the future, products that are usable by all people in the community. Indeed, there are defined principles relating to this concept (North Carolina State University, 1997; Vanderheiden, 1998). There has always been a need for specific assistive technologies – some people have very severe disabilities and it is unrealistic to expect a mainstream personal computer manufacturer to provide everything to assist such people (for example, puff and blow as an interface, or a switch in, and so forth). COST 219 (a European Commission Action on Telecommunications and Disability[9]) suggests three levels to universal design: make as many products as accessible as possible; connect assistive technology and mainstream equipment; and provide appropriate assistive technology (COST 219, 2001).

A final barrier, often cited as the most important, is the negative societal view of disability. Identifying and understanding the heterogeneity of assistive technology users enables libraries and other service providers to develop a range of resources and services to meet the diverse needs of assistive technology users. With the identification of issues and support strategies for assistive technology use in society, appropriate measures can be implemented to ensure that the spirit of disability discrimination legislation actually enables people with disabilities to be integrated into society.

The most recent major change has been the advent of the new wireless technology. This wireless (or wi-fi) technology affords unbridled power to connect and the freedom to move. As wireless technologies continue to evolve, the future will be definitely wireless, and the potential of wireless technology for people with disabilities presents opportunities for freedom to be 'sensed' and physical limitations to be continuously challenged and shifted. To realise this promise fully, developers must embrace the concepts of universal design.

The future – improving information services

Goggin and Newell (2003) remind us that recent developments in ICT are commonly regarded as the panacea for persons with physical disabilities. This is because the technology can give people with disabilities access to the total virtual world and many aspects of the real world previously inaccessible to them. Therefore, the technology has the capacity to be empowering for people with disabilities (Shearman, 1999: 3; Sheldon, 2003). However, we need to be ever mindful 'that in whatever we do we have the opportunity to disable or enable' (Goggin and Newell, 2003: 154):

> In different accents and voices, we are ceaselessly promised that technology will deliver us from disability. Yet we would suggest not only that technology will never deliver society from the reality of disability, but that disability continues to be constructed through such technology. As a socio-political space, disability will continue to exist, and technology will remain an important site in which it is constructed (Goggin and Newell, 2003: 153).

Extensive IT development and society's capacity to embrace technological change mean that people with disabilities can participate where factors over which they themselves have control are the main limits to their connectivity.

Ultimately, access to ICT and information/libraries for persons with disabilities are contingent on acceptance, affordability, usability, and the adoption of universal design principles in equipment and in information format. Great opportunities and immense challenges lie ahead. All stakeholders need to be challenged to develop strategies and initiatives to foster a collaborative approach to problem resolution that will be of value (and impact) for people with disabilities in this global world.

Notes

1. The International Alliance of Assistive Technology Information Providers has used the term since 2003, when a Memorandum of Understanding was signed to increase knowledge sharing and networking internally. Organisations from Italy, Denmark, Germany, Great Britain, Spain, USA, Holland and France are part of the alliance (see *http://portale.siva.it/servizi/iaatip/default_eng.asp*).

2. Rehabtool.com provides a comprehensive list of assistive technology products for specific disabilities. Ability Hub provides information about adaptive technology for accessing computers. Tech Assist On-line is an Australian service for assistive technology for computers (hardware, software and ergonomic equipment that makes a computer easier to use; see *http://www.techassist.org.au*).

3. An adaptive and assistive technologies report has recently been released in Australia (see *http://www.ngo.net.au/communitynet/index.php?option=content&task=view&id=8783&Itemid=2*).

4. The Australian Rehabilitation and Assistive Technology Association (ARATA) was formed in 1995 to serve as a national forum on relevant rehabilitation technology issues. They hold regular conferences.

5. It is worth noting that the distribution of the 2001 Paraplegic and Quadriplegic Association of Queensland Member Survey was available online, or by using paper and pencil, facsimile and by post. Thirty per cent of the responses were returned online from public libraries. A mere two years after the last survey, almost 90 per cent of respondents reported that they had access to both the Internet and e-mail, which represents a significant difference to the 20 per cent reported two years previously. However, by the 2003 member's survey, this had reduced to only 51 per cent of respondents having access to both Internet and e-mail. This reduction in access and use of ICT might link to the fact that the majority of respondents (38.8 per cent) indicated receiving the Disability Support Pension, while now only 32 per cent of respondents indicated having employment of some kind.

6. The Australian Government Department of Communication, Information Technology and the Arts has commissioned the Allen Consulting Group (*http://www.allenconsult.com.au*) to undertake a review of the Disability Equipment Program and to present their findings. Part of their brief is to conduct small focus groups of consumers who use the programme. They also are consulting with advocacy groups, regulators and equipment providers.

7. The double-edged sword refers to a small but growing body of work within disability studies that emphasises technology's 'doubled-edged nature' (Oliver, 1990) and stresses that it can be 'both oppressive and emancipatory, depending on the social uses to which it is put' (Gleeson, 1999: 104, in Sheldon, 2003).

8. This access through TADAust Connect ISP (*http://www .tadaustconnect.org.au*) is a low-cost dial-up service with no set-up fee and no limit on downloads, no connection or disconnection fee and is a local connect call (toll-free Australia wide). TADAust also offers broadband service and is specifically targeted to serve people with disabilities, older people and veterans.

9. COST (*http://www.stakes.fi/cost219/*) is a framework for scientific and technical cooperation in Europe, the main aspect of which is the coordination of national research on a European level. The COST cooperation consists of the European Commission, the 15 EU member states and ten non-member states. COST is based on a flexible set of arrangements enabling different national organisations, institutes, universities and industry to join forces and make concerted efforts in a broad range of scientific and technical areas.

5

Reaching people with disabilities in developing countries through academic libraries

Ayo Onatola

Introduction

According to the United Nations Development Programme (UNDP), about 10 per cent of the world's population have disabilities. Especially in developing countries, these people face physical and attitudinal barriers, which contribute to their isolation and impoverishment. The prevalence of disability in many developing countries is further compounded by the fact that there is a lack of appropriate and comparable data on which to hinge most policy formulations (Peters, 2003). If development is the expansion of (and removal of barriers to) the freedoms that people enjoy, a key aspect will be to improve access to the environment by people with disabilities (Wirz and Meikle, 2005). Academic libraries are poised to be at the fore of these efforts.

Academic libraries help actualise the mission of their parent colleges or universities. Libraries complement teaching, training and learning activities in the institutions. They strive to ensure that the instruction and research needs of the faculty and students are adequately met. Hence, their collections (textbooks, serials, non-prints, etc.) support the implementation of the curricula, while extensive reference materials are also provided to aid in-depth research. How far they support maximising access to people with disabilities in developing countries forms the crux of this chapter.

This chapter uses as a model an evaluative study carried out in the libraries of 24 (of 43 total) Nigerian universities, comprising 21 federal, 18 state and four privately-owned institutions from the six Nigerian geopolitical zones. Academic libraries were evaluated for their adherence to extant governmental policies, and to establish the extent of their preparations for coping with the varying and specialised needs of people with disabilities.

From the responses obtained on the current state of affairs in Nigerian academic libraries, there is little cheering to write about. Services in most are archaic and at the verge of being moribund due to government insensitivities and under-funding. Neglect in the provision of required facilities to support people with disabilities is especially disheartening.

At the same time, there are possibilities of reversing the present state, improving on the weaknesses in the system and proffering appropriate measures to address the anomalies identified. These strategies would improve the Nigerian system and would serve as a model of implementing the ideals of good library practice, and will help librarians meet the general and special needs of all categories of patrons of academic libraries in developing nations.

What constitutes disability?

For the purposes of this discussion, disability is described using the World Health Organization's International

Classification of Impairments, Disabilities and Handicaps (1980):

> Impairment is any loss or abnormality of psychological, physiological, and anatomical nature, structure or/and functions. Disability, describes any restriction or lack (resulting from an impairment) of ability to perform an activity in the manner or within the range considered normal for a human being. Handicap could be taken as a disadvantage for a given individual, resulting from an impairment or disability, thereby limiting or preventing the easy fulfilment of a role (depending on age, sex, social or cultural factors).[1]

The implication of this is that a person with a disability will be unable to be active in many routine activities including working and learning. These assumptions, combined with longstanding social prejudice, help explain the preponderance of people with disabilities in the lowest education and income levels of society in developing nations (Onwuegbu, 1977). For too many, begging for alms is the only survival option. Inadequate mobility, architectural barriers and poverty prevent them from participating fully in basic elementary education. Those who do graduate often are deprived access to higher education not because of their being found wanting in intellectual ability but as a result of structural obstacles. More often than not, people with disabilities are steered to technical colleges where they receive vocational training for a future trading activity.

Nigerian academic libraries are plagued with many physical barriers. Most public buildings in Nigeria are only accessible by stairs; the pavements near many buildings are in disrepair or even completely lacking. There is no equivalent to laws like the UK Disabilities Discrimination Act 1995 or the Americans with Disabilities Act 1990. Furthermore, in most cases there are no funds for building reconstruction.

Government policies in developing countries: the example of Nigeria

Nigeria is the most populous and richest oil-producing country in Africa, and is seemingly poised to support educational inclusion. Yet, attitudes of government stakeholders to funding education, especially as it relates to promoting education among people with disabilities, hinders progress in achieving full access.

The major notable change in the Nigerian educational system in post-independence 1960s up to the early 1970s was the proliferation of primary and secondary schools, colleges of education, and polytechnics. In addition, the first generation of federally-funded universities was established during this period. The post-civil war period, beginning around 1970, witnessed some facelifting of education standards as a part of the First National Development Plan. Perceived inequalities in the federal university quota system and a desire to protect the interests of youth from 'educationally advanced' states in turn led to the emergence of state-owned universities in the 1980s.

The most noticeable effort of the government around 1975–80 relating to the education of people with disabilities, was the enactment of Section 8 of the National Policy on Education (1977), which gives such guidelines for the achievement of stable programmes in special education as listed below:

- to give concrete meaning to the idea of equalising educational opportunities for all children, their physical and emotional disabilities notwithstanding;

- to provide adequate education for all 'handicapped' children and adults in order that they may fully play their roles in the development of the nation;

- to provide opportunities for exceptionally gifted children to develop at their own pace in the interest of the nation's economic and technological development.

Unfortunately, activists have not been able to make these guidelines a national law to date. Further, the millions of naira purportedly allocated to education in yearly budgets have not yielded significant dividends, as they are too often directed to politically-motivated 'elephant' projects from which the masses rarely benefit. Other prominent studies carried out in Nigeria especially by Atinmo (1979), Ihunnah (1984), Oluigbo (1986, 1990), Bakare (1992), Obiakor, Bragg and Maltby (1993) and the Association of Libraries for the Visually Impaired (ALVI) implicate the lip service given by the various tiers of government to issues of education of people of school age and with disabilities, especially the ill-equipping of libraries. This lack of a willingness to make a formal national commitment to inclusive education continues to pose tremendous problems for the realisation of education reform in Nigeria.

Education of people with disabilities in Nigeria

The education and future of people with disabilities appears somewhat bleak so long as Section 8 remains as a theoretical document, not backed by any legislation. The practical result for universities is that no special consideration is given to providing hostel accommodation, offices, cafeterias, classrooms, laboratories and libraries that are accessible to students with disabilities. Where required equipment and facilities are procured, they are based on people with disabilities remaining in their current role only, without anticipating future needs or emerging situations.

Individual cases revealed in our survey are illustrative. For example, a student in his fourth year of a six-year medical programme lost one of his limbs in a car accident, and a female student athlete, suffered a part-paralysis in a sporting accident. In neither case did university authorities encourage these people to continue their studies; rather they allowed them to drop out unremarked.

A similar reluctance to accommodate disability has been seen with staff, as in another case concerning a staff member who was made redundant after suffering brain damage following surgery during labour. As a result of instances like these, the university – and the country – lost valuable contributors, as the affected individuals lost their careers and futures.

Regrettably, many special education placements in Nigerian primary and post-primary schools have not resulted in the desired maximisation of individuals' potential. Students with disabilities still are commonly institutionalised, leading to segregation that hampers both their self-perception and their ability to succeed in mainstream society (Atinmo and Dawha, 1997). The segregation continues, with students separated by specific disability. Examples include various schools 'for the handicapped', 'for the deaf', 'for the blind', or 'of special education'. While a specialist school might be best for a specific child, pupils' individual needs are often neglected; for example, almost all deaf children are simply referred to a school for the deaf. Making the situation worse, such schools are only within the financial and geographic reach of children and wards of affluent families.

As a result, poor children with disabilities suffer deprivation and commonly receive no education whatsoever.

The efforts of some non-governmental organisations and a few public institutions that are at the forefront of computer Braille production in Nigeria deserve recognition. Examples of such bodies are the Nigerwives (Association of Foreign Wives of Nigerians) Braille Book Production Centre, Falomo, Lagos (also the Kings College Annexe, Victoria Island, Lagos); the Anglo-Nigerian Welfare Association for the Blind (ANWAB), Commercial Avenue, Sabo, Yaba-Lagos; the Pacelli School for the Blind, Yaba-Lagos, Lagos State; Gindiri School for the Blind, Barkin-Ladi, via Jos; and the Department of Special Education, University of Jos, Plateau State. These NGOs and other institutions cooperate by procuring the same reproduction and translation equipment so that they can exchange master copies that can be made available in various libraries, avoiding the time and cost of duplicating the same materials.

The receipt of some Braille books in the past years from the Library of Congress and further distribution by Nigerwives, ANWAB and the Inlaks Library of the Vocational Training Centre, Oshodi is noteworthy. Nevertheless, it remains impossible for these establishments to meet the demand for reading materials by people with visual impairments especially at university level. As an exception, the authorities of those universities where special education is offered will collaborate with or provide funds to groups, thereby procuring the required equipment for libraries to assist their patrons who have disabilities.[2]

In sum, this educational background provides the base from which universities and academic libraries draw their students. Those students with disabilities who do enter university are more likely to come from an affluent, supportive background. They also are certain to have overcome significant physical, structural and attitudinal barriers in achieving academic success.[3]

The impact of academic libraries on people with disabilities

In 2006, while exploring the possibility of a computerised catalogue and distribution database of alternative materials for the visually impaired in Nigeria, ALVI noted that hundreds of blind pupils attended primary and secondary schools, whereas their population at higher institutions is very insignificant. ALVI linked the small disabled population in universities to the observed shortage of specialised learning materials, such as talking books and Braille, available at lower levels but not in academic libraries.

The situation is not unique to Nigeria. Ochoggia (2003) gave a predictive exposition on the possible roles that libraries and information centres can play to support the visually handicapped in Kenya while analysing the Kenyan Persons with Disability Bill 2000. Crouse (2004) lamented the unmet needs of students with disabilities and the discrimination against them, in contradiction to the provision in the Constitution of the Republic of South Africa in promoting equity among all people, specifically including those with disabilities. Runhare (2004) catalogued inequitable access to education in a study carried out on institutions in Zimbabwe. Currently, in most developing nations, the policies on special education remain operationally inclusive (UNESCO, 2005b), promoting inclusion over segregation. However, much work must be done for inclusion to be achievable.[4]

Emerging library initiatives

For many decades, the World Bank and other international agencies have promoted educational development, especially capacity building, worldwide. There is an ongoing effort towards ensuring that library services are within the reach of people with disabilities in developing countries (World Bank, 2006). In addition, a relatively new strategy known as 'community based rehabilitation' (CBR) implemented by some developing countries to improve the quality of life of people with disabilities through health services (Mendis, 1989), could also be introduced to the education sector. CBR strives to ensure that individuals, communities and society accept the equal rights of individuals with disabilities to have full access to information sources. As applied to libraries, it will be aimed at ensuring that people with disabilities are able to maximise their physical and mental abilities, to access regular services and opportunities, and to become active contributors to the community and society at large. CBR underscores the United Nations Standard Rules on the Equalization of Opportunities for Persons with Disabilities, which require countries to ensure adequate training of all personnel concerned with the planning and execution of programmes and services provision meant for people with disabilities (WHO, 2006).

In this age of information explosion, university libraries can be instrumental to breaking the existing barriers preventing easy access to library materials by people with disabilities. By participating in global initiatives such as CBR, librarians can involve university administrators and promote in-service training to library professionals. They can help administrators and library staff alike understand the importance of using newly-acquired knowledge and skills to strengthen the achievements of people with disabilities by maximising their capabilities.

In Nigeria, achievement of positive outcomes from initiatives such as CBR and other intervention models requires more emphasis on funding special education. In addition, governments and academic institutions in developing nations must understand the value of prioritising policy formulation and project execution. As an example of the type of initiative that should be encouraged, various tiers of government may grant inducements in the form of allowances to help students and staff with disabilities to meet up with any additional cost while undergoing higher education. For example, staff with mobility problems can be assisted through loans to enable them procure wheelchairs or other mobility aids.

The respective universities can also lend academic support to people with disabilities to access the course materials they need easily by providing the required specialised equipment in their dormitories, lecture rooms and libraries. Library administrators should endeavour to hire librarians with a first degree in special education or disability studies, who have an in-depth understanding of how to satisfy the information and educational needs of students with disabilities (Pinfield, 2001). These librarians can provide aid directly to patrons and can also train other staff on how to use adaptive technology on computers and standalone systems, and how to provide effective and appropriate advisory/reference services.

Library architecture

The present situation in all universities in Nigeria is such that students and staff who use wheelchairs must literally be carried when they want to access public facilities such as lecture rooms and libraries. Unfortunately, most university administrators view building ramps at the library as a luxury, so sloppy temporary ramps (without supporting rails) are the only access points, too often leading to doors too heavy for many people to open. In some university libraries, elevators are out of use due to lack of maintenance or are simply abandoned at construction stage due to lack of funds. Hence, the alternative arrangement made is to restrict users of wheelchairs to the ground floor, regardless of where needed materials are housed. There are no formal paging services, and the students must rely on friends to source and retrieve the needed materials from upper floors.

When a new building is designed, it should incorporate universal design features to promote access for all individuals. University librarians need to conduct physical access audits, evaluate needs and ensure proper funding of the required physical alterations in buildings, procurement of special equipment, and staff training to make things work for the benefit of all their patrons, including those with disabilities.

Librarians working in older facilities and with limited funds still can make changes to improve access. For a typical university library, access could be improved simply by installing a stable ramp leading to an automatic or easily opened main entrance at the ground level, with an intercom to contact library staff if assistance is needed. An accessible study area including a computer station and workspace should be nearby. Where there are lifts, audible signals or audio recordings can be used to indicate on which floor the elevator might be. Where there is no elevator service, library staff should be trained to offer to page books for patrons who have mobility impairments. In addition, a classroom, conference room, or similar facility should be accessible for holding programmes where people with mobility impairments are in attendance. Clear, prominent signage also can help people use the library independently. Restrooms, if not designed for wheelchair users, can be improved by keeping them clear of clutter, with floors clean and dry. To facilitate parking, bays close to the library can be marked out clearly and reserved for those who need them.

Available equipment and services

In general, there are no adequate provisions for people who need adaptive technology or alternative materials. Some academic libraries in Nigeria do have Braille production facilities, and in other schools there are departments of special education that cater to students with physical disabilities.

In some cases, the existence of specialised, segregated libraries can be a problem in itself. For example, The Kenneth Dike Library, University of Ibadan, which arguably has the largest research-level collection in the country, still refers patrons with visual impairments to places like the Oyo State Library Board, Dugbe-Ibadan – a public library with functional Braille services. Similarly, people with mental and learning disabilities are often referred to the libraries of the Psychiatric Hospital Yaba, Lagos and/or the Neuro-psychiatric Specialist Hospital, Aro, Abeokuta, based on their disabilities, rather than their subject needs.

A typical academic library can provide equipment to lend adequate support to research, training, teaching and learning activities of the parent institution it serves. Many of these tools are free or at very low cost. Librarians also can apply for grants to cover more expensive equipment:

- literacy software such as TextHELP Read and Write that can help with spelling, proof reading and can read text out loud;
- mind-mapping/idea-mapping software such as Inspiration and MindGenius that can be used to create idea-maps or tree diagrams to help students plan essays, reports or presentations or make revision notes;
- screen magnification software to enlarge text and images displayed on the computer screen;
- synthetic speech software such as JAWS that reads the screen contents aloud;

- reading-edge or similar scanners that use OCR technology to scan and read printed material to the user;

- radio frequency (RF) transmitter or inductive loop systems to allow people with hearing aids to take advantage of audio presentations;

- bar magnifier/magnifying sheet to provide low (generally 2–5×) magnification of printed text;

- CCTV or similar enlarging machine, for viewing books and other printed materials, in either stationary or portable models;

- MP3, CD, and/or cassette player for listening to and recording lectures, etc. or to listen to audio books.

When limited equipment is available, an equipment loan pool can be established. This provides one central source where library users can obtain accessibility aids and adaptive equipment.

Librarians also can help by being aware of features already built into computers and audiovisual materials. For example, Windows has numerous accessibility options that can benefit people with visual impairments and fine motor skills. In addition, many DVDs are close-captioned – librarians need only turn on the captioning to make these accessible to people with hearing impairments. Similarly, a small but growing number of DVDs are now including descriptive captioning that provides audio narration of visual elements so that people with visual impairments can better enjoy them.

Librarians also can assist by being aware of the barriers within their libraries and proactively helping patrons who need assistance. No-cost solutions to maximising service include paging books, providing personal research assistance, helping users with computer enquiries, and making sure that accessible parking, study areas and restrooms are kept free for use by the people who need them. Suggested service solutions when materials, equipment or facilities are not accessible are provided below:

- *Home library service*: when staff or students cannot get to the library, a librarian, preferably a subject specialist in the student/faculty member's area of research, will visit. The librarian will establish what kinds of material they require and in what format. The librarian can establish a delivery schedule, and will remain as the person's primary point of contact for reference and research questions. Actual delivery of material can be done through inter-office mail or by support staff or student volunteers.

- *Extended loan periods*: students with disabilities can be granted extended loan periods for reserve items and bound periodicals, subject to other demands on the material. Renewal of library materials via phone or e-mail, even where not allowed for students without disabilities, should be considered.

- *Interlibrary loan services (ILS) and networking for special materials*: as previously noted, there are consortia in place for lending Braille materials in Nigeria and in other countries. Use of these should be encouraged and university library patrons should be trained to use union catalogues and make ILS requests via traditional forms, by phone, or using tools such as ILLiad, an automated request system available via the Internet.

- *Printing and photocopying of documents*: under 'fair use', pages of books and journals can be printed at cost for individual use without violating copyright laws. Students who have vision impairments also may obtain large print copies (via photocopying) at the same flat rate for a regular size. It may be possible to make arrangements for this service in person at the library, or to have the student/faculty member phone ahead so the material can be prepared in advance.

- *Information location tools*: a guide to using the library, its services, and electronic aids such as the online catalogue and other research tools should be created by every university library. Copies should be distributed to all students, staff and faculty, and be available online in an accessible format.

- *Library tours and instruction*: regular tours and introductions covering general information about library resources should be offered to interested students and staff. In addition, special tours can be arranged for students to identify any special accommodations or equipment they may need.

- *Conspicuous guides and signage to promote independent library use*: as some patrons may not have visible disabilities, guides providing basic service and access information for people with disabilities should be conspicuously exhibited in each library. Similarly, signage should be clear, and maps should show all designated parking, accessible building entrances, accessible restrooms and locations of adaptive equipment. Guides and signs should use the standard symbols of accessibility to connote wheelchair-accessible routes and facilities; these can be downloaded from *http://www.gag.org/ resources/das.php* and other Internet sites.

Other initiatives to improve academic library services

As promoters of learning communities, libraries are encouraged to form 'pressure groups' to help connect all stakeholders (individuals with disabilities, friends and colleagues, and academic/library representatives) concerned with disability issues. These groups can help advocate for improved services and can promote awareness on the campus. To demonstrate a formal commitment to these ideas, every university library should include in its statutes and regulations a clause that prohibits discrimination against people with disabilities and promotes equitable service.

Every academic library should strive to have a distinct section or, for smaller libraries, a liaison to cater to any special needs of people with disabilities. Such a section is best headed by a trained library professional with related subject background in special education or disability studies. This section or liaison can help all categories of users; advocating for appropriate collection development; selecting adaptive equipment; and carrying out staff skills training for a greater involvement in service provision.

Library professionals in developing nations also must continue liaising with their colleagues in sister university libraries and relevant organisations, both locally and internationally. Such networks help establish appropriate and modern methods of best practice, and provide real-world teams to make their services accessible to people with disabilities. Networking also allows academic libraries in developing countries to emulate their counterparts in advanced nations by offering services that demonstrate an acceptance of students and staff with disabilities within 'town and gown' communities, the country, and the world at large.

Conclusions

The barriers linked to inadequacies in physical infrastructures, collections and facilities/equipment, inadequately trained librarians, and a lack of funding of university libraries in Nigeria and other developing nations combine to inhibit access to libraries and higher education, by people with disabilities. Architects, planners and builders must consider how to design the physical environment so that people with disabilities can fully use facilities and take part in activities of their choice (Wirz and Meikle, 2005). Library funders must prioritise acquisition of the hardware and software needed by people with disabilities to be able to study, teach and conduct research (Mates, 2000). Libraries should press for more transparent commitment and determination to improve conditions of people with disabilities on the part of government, rather than leaving everything to private individuals and non-governmental organisations. Library professionals also need to look inward to promote an attitude that maximises the use of resources at hand in serving patrons who have disabilities.

Approaches to ensuring access to academic libraries for people with disabilities will vary among and within countries; however, it will be in the best interest of developing nations to emulate the drives of the advanced countries. With a workable policy backing up the protection of rights of the people with disabilities, librarianship can further its reputation as a profession based on the ethics of equity of information access. Decisive action implemented with practical steps can guide operating procedures. Increased attention can begin to be accorded to the needs of people with disabilities in general society while more research is conducted to better define issues, interventions and outcomes. The result will be greater contributions to society by a segment of the population too long denied the opportunity to reach its full potential.

Notes

1. For further information on this document, see the American Speech-Language-Hearing Association's article 'Impairment, disorder, disability', available at: *http://www.asha.org/public/ hearing/disorders/impair_dis_disab.htm*. The meaning of 'disability' and 'disabled person' are also defined in the UK Disability Discrimination Act 1995, Part I, Chapter 50. (*http://www.opsi.gov.uk/acts/acts1995/95050--a.htm#1*) and the US Americans with Disabilities Act 1990 (*http://www .adapts.gatech.edu/faculty_guide/ada.htm*).
2. Danlami (2000) also addresses collaboration successes and challenges.
3. For more information on special education, see Abang (1992) and Mba (2000).
4. Additional sources on academic library access may be found in Harris and Oppenheim (2003), Jones and Tedd (2003) and McNulty (1999).

6

Finding the means to improve services

Young Sook Lee

Introduction

During the past two decades, one of the top political issues in any society has been the integration of people with disabilities into mainstream society. Led by the proclamation of the UN's International Year of Disabled Persons (IYDP) in 1981, nations have formulated various legal frameworks to prevent people who have disabilities from being discriminated against or excluded from work. Recognising their rights, people with disabilities are taking joint actions and requesting that society allow them full participation and equal opportunities in education, employment and community activities – the same as their able-bodied counterparts enjoy. Thus, especially in the last two decades, we have witnessed the challenges and responses between people with disabilities and society on many issues of full integration.

Libraries are part of society and reflect social trends. Making mainstream library services accessible for people with disabilities has been required through enactment of anti-discrimination acts in many countries. This chapter discusses various issues related to the integration of people who have disabilities into mainstream library services. The first part focuses on legal aspects of anti-discrimination acts and the abilities of people with disabilities that challenge mainstream libraries to open their doors to them. The second part focuses on good examples of library service to people with disabilities throughout the world. This is discussed in the context of the development of technology, which is regarded as the most significant factor to bring changes in services as well as a key tool for integrating library services for people with disabilities into the mainstream. The third part focuses on obstacles faced by libraries when they offer services for people with disabilities. These are the mainly invisible psychological barriers caused by librarians' attitudes towards disabled people, and the dearth of librarians' knowledge and experiences in characteristics of disabilities and people with disabilities. Combined, these have the most negative impact on the integration of people into mainstream libraries.

Abilities of people with disabilities

The theme of the 1981 IYDP was 'Full-participation and Equality'. Undoubtedly, the designation of this year played a great role in creating a new image of disability and in changing the general public's attitudes towards people who have disabilities. As a result, governments in many countries have implemented policies on integration of people with disabilities into mainstream society, especially in education, employment, services, programmes etc. In 1990, the Americans with Disabilities Act (ADA) was enacted in the USA, followed by the Disability Discrimination Act 1992 in Australia and the Disability Discrimination Act 1995 (DDA) in the UK. In South Korea, although there is no anti-discrimination act per se, in 1997 the government enacted the Act on Installation of Convenience Facilities for the Disabled. The purpose of the Act is to increase the participation of disabled people in society and to improve social welfare by enabling them to make use of facilities and equipment safely and conveniently, and to access information independently.

In addition to anti-discrimination acts, since 1970 there has been a strong trend of integration for children with disabilities into mainstream schools in many countries. Mainstream schools mean general schools in which non-disabled children are taught. Under the term 'mainstreaming', children with disabilities have been placed in general classes or special classes in mainstream schools. In South Korea, pioneers in education had a strong belief that children with disabilities are not different from those without disabilities and should be taught at mainstream schools. They tried hard to legalise the integration of disabled children into the mainstream sector from the late 1960s. In their view, the integration of education was seen as the first step of full social integration of people with disabilities. They have met with some success. Currently in South Korea, following the 1997 Special Education Promotion Law, principals of general schools should admit children who need special education when requested by the students themselves, parents or principals of special schools.

Through improved integration of education, many people with disabilities have been able to develop their potential and to live with financial independence. Moreover, they understand their rights and have become aware that the only way to improve the status quo is to organise themselves. Setting up their own organisations, people with disabilities have started taking joint actions to address the issues concerning their welfare and future.

Numerous stories related to joint actions show the abilities of people with disabilities throughout the world. For example, in Britain since 1982 there were 13 unsuccessful attempts to get anti-discrimination legislation through Parliament before the enactment of the DDA. Activists argued that legislation should emphasise civil rights rather than individual needs and should focus on the society in which people live, not upon individual people with disabilities. In the USA, there is a similar story behind the enactment of the ADA. The ADA is considered by many to be the most significant civil rights legislation passed by the US federal government since the Civil Rights Act 1964.

It is interesting to note the connections with disability of many of the politicians in the USA closely associated with the ADA. For example, President George Bush, who signed the legislation, has two sons with disabilities; Edward Kennedy, a Senate supporter of the ADA, has a sister with learning difficulties and a son who lost a leg to cancer; Senator Lowell Weicker, Jr, has a child with Down's syndrome; Senator Bob Dole has a paralysed right arm; the chief Senate sponsor, Tom Harkin, has a deaf brother and a nephew who is paralysed. A congressman who was one of the chief sponsors of the bill remarked in a speech at a banquet that disability affects practically every family.

In South Korea, one of the best-known figures advocating for the full integration of people with disabilities is Dr Young Woo Kang. Dr Kang, who is blind, marks among his accomplishments service as Vice Chairman of the World Committee on Disability, member of the National Council on Disabilities in the United States, and Senior Adviser for the Roosevelt Institute. A television drama, *A Light in my Heart*, based on a true story of Kang's boyhood, produced by Munhaw Broadcasting Company (MBC), was played at the Headquarters of United Nations on the International

Disabled Persons Day on 3rd December 1995. In 1996, eight months after the drama aired, South Korea became the first country to be awarded the first Roosevelt International Disability Award, partly due to Dr Kang's efforts. South Korea was unanimously selected as the first winner after heated discussions. Then-President Kim Young Sam received the award on behalf of his country.

The award had a significant effect. After receiving the award, the South Korean government immediately took measures to improve the standard of disabled people's lives. Two remarkable measures were the enactment of the Act on Installation of Convenience Facilities for the Disabled 1997 and enactment of the improvement of Special Education Promotion Law in 1997. In addition, the government dramatically increased the budget for social welfare and education for people with disabilities.

Both the US and South Korean examples show the power of individuals, organisations and activists to play a constructive role in building society as a result of pursuing full civil rights for people with disabilities. There are accounts of this kind in improving the library sector as well. In Denmark, for example, press groups of disabled people influenced the government to enact two pieces of legislation: the Danish Public Library Act 1994 and the Danish Copyright Act 1995. In the Danish Public Library Act, it is legally established that talking books are treated on equal terms with printed books in the interlibrary lending system. In the Danish Copyright Act, the transmission of electronic texts from The Danish National Library for the Blind to blind people is legalised. These two acts are probably the most distinguished laws for the benefit of disabled library users in the world. The enactment of these two laws also illustrates the political strength of people with disabilities in Denmark. A librarian at the conference noted that in

Denmark, blind people are not considered to be a 'weak' group in society. Quite the contrary, blind people have managed to attract political attention through their strong organisation and lobbying efforts. Thus, even when library budgets are cut, it is rare that services benefiting people who are blind are affected.

In South Korea in 2003, one of the hot political issues was the formulation of an anti-discrimination act. For this matter, a special team was established in April, 2003. All disability-related associations, institutions and agencies in South Korea stood together and demanded equal opportunity and full participation in education, employment, access, and social and cultural activities, etc. Unlike in the past, disabled people are no longer bystanders with respect to legislation affecting their interests. They have attempted to draft an act by themselves and have campaigned for it to become law. In 2005, the team formulated the Disabled Persons Discrimination Prohibition Law, which they are now waiting for the National Assembly to enact. Using the act as tool with which to fight, they will challenge libraries in South Korea to offer services to people with disabilities.

Library service initiatives for people with disabilities

An American public library director, Marsha Werle, has said:

> It is shameful that is has to take a law to get businesses, schools, and libraries to comply with standards of excellence for those with disabilities. However, law can give librarians a tool to bring to our library boards to

> promote change through remodeling, materials,
> equipment, signage, and attitude. (Werle, 2003)

When the board of trustees and the staff of the library where
she works sought to comply with the ADA in 1990, they
asked themselves what they could do with little or no
money. Their first achievement was handicapped parking
spaces in their two parking lots that were provided free by
their municipality. They also installed an inexpensive,
battery-operated doorbell on their front door for those who
might need assistance in opening doors. They replaced
doorknob handles throughout the library with lever handles
by obtaining used commercial handles at about half the cost
of new. Two members of their community who died willed
the library magnification equipment to amplify images of
printed materials. These were used not only for books, but
also by people with reduced vision to read prescription
bottles, write cheques and examine photographs. As a result,
the library has seen slow but steady gains in services for
people with disabilities. As an example, the library now has
on average at least one patron each day who uses a
wheelchair – ten years ago, they had an average of two
wheelchair users each year.

Whether or not anti-discrimination laws exist, there are
many library professionals who have recognised their ethical
imperative to reach disabled users. These librarians have
tried to offer complete access to information resources for
all patrons. For instance, the Manchester Central Library in
the UK first planned to purchase a Kurzweil Reading
Machine to provide services for visually impaired people in
1982. As the machine was extremely expensive, it was likely
that very few blind people would be able to purchase one for
their own use; as such the Library was convinced that the
equipment should be provided by a public institution.

Although no law required it, they commenced their services in the belief that the most appropriate public institution to have a reading machine was that which held the materials to read. David Owen, who was Director of Libraries in Manchester at that time, told the Library Association in Britain how the Kurzweil reading machine was acquired:

> Our decision a year ago to provide a library service for the 16,500 registered blind and partially sighted people in the Greater Manchester area for the first time was taken in half an hour – all that was needed for the Kurzweil reading machine to prove that it can convert ordinary printed material, books, periodicals, reports and typewritten materials into synthetic speech ... In that prophetic half-hour we heard and understood it reading material ranging from specialist local history books published in the nineteenth century to a history of Manchester United Football Club.

The benefits were immediately obvious, but they faced a major problem finding the money to purchase at least one. The prevailing financial situation was grim and there was no possibility of obtaining the required £23,000 through normal channels. So they launched a public appeal, and to apply to the UK Department of the Environment (DoE) for assistance through its Urban Aid Programme. With the aid of the public and local companies, through the appeal, and with DoE assistance they were able to raise enough funds to order two machines and took delivery of them in March 1983.

Consequent media attention to the Manchester Library was inevitable. Staff known by this author reported how pleased they were when their friends and relatives applauded the merits of this service, having seen it on BBC Television's news. The news boosted staff morale at all levels.

In South Korea, several public libraries offered services for the visually impaired by combining forces and setting up a special unit in the 1980s. These special units produce alternative materials, including Braille and talking books, for people with visual impairments. Many volunteers involved in the production delivered materials in person or mailed them to visually impaired users.

Among the public libraries, Hwadojin Library, located in the metropolitan city of Incheon, has an especially popular unit. Sook Kyoung Whang, head of the unit, previously worked for the South Korea Braille Library, and has initiated various programmes, mainly focusing on children with disabilities. Most of the programmes for children she developed, such as 'Music Class under One Mind' and 'Summer and Winter Reading Class', were designed to put children with and without disabilities in activities together. She has a strong belief in the philosophy that children with disabilities can develop their potential and use their abilities spontaneously through participating in integrated programmes. She also believes that through the programmes, children without disabilities are able to recognise the abilities of their peers with disabilities.

As with the Manchester example, the unit's success has been partially driven by an ability to secure funding. The unit continually tracks funding opportunities and sources. Proposals are submitted directly following the official announcement of any new available sponsorship from institutions or agencies. Sook Kyoung Whang's tactic to winning grants is to be persistent, trying different angles if the first attempt has not hit the target. She also frequently participates in community meetings to collect information and share experiences, and her name is well known outside the library. As a result, she has been able to secure funding for almost every initiative proposed by the unit.

Information technology as an opportunity for mainstream libraries

As anti-discrimination acts challenge mainstream libraries to open their doors to the disabled, information technology also has accelerated the improvement of library services for the disabled. In general, the development of library services for people with disabilities has paralleled the development of new technology. This has played a significant role in the increase of library membership, particularly among the print disabled – people who for whatever reason have difficulty reading standard printed text. In the 1930s, the advent of talking books served as a milestone in the progress of library services for the visually impaired. Before the production of talking books, Braille had been used as a major reading format for the blind. Braille is read by using fingertips, thus requires sensitivity in the fingertips. People who have lost eyesight in the later stages of life and have not learned Braille from a relatively early age have great difficulty in reading it. This can be compounded if they have lost sensitivity in their fingertips already. As a result, talking books have become an invaluable reading method for visually impaired people, especially senior citizens. Talking books also benefit those who have physical difficulty holding books or turning pages.

In the current era of electronic information, even totally blind people can use assistive software to access computer catalogues, electronic books and journals, and literally worldwide information resources through the Internet. Electronic information gives people with visual impairments two fundamental freedoms – independence and choice. Previously, all reading materials for visually impaired people had to be converted into large print, Braille or talking books. To supplement these sources, people with blindness or reduced vision had to ask others to read materials to them. All of these processes required human intervention and time – hours, weeks or even years. By facilitating speedy and independent access to information, technology provides opportunity to mainstream libraries to promote services to people with disabilities.

In addition, there is a significant interest from public libraries around the world in connecting to the Internet and providing new services for their communities. For example, in 1999 when in Britain the Islington Central Library in London launched the accessible Internet services for visually impaired people for the first time, Education Secretary David Blunkett, who is blind, came to offer his support. Among the benefits cited for the project were new opportunities for people with visual impairments to continue their studies and personal development, to improve their independence, to shop, surf, or simply to talk to others.

The cost of the accessible Internet service project was only £2,700, of which £1,500 was provided as a grant by the Ulverscroft Large Print Book Company. Alan Issler, Principal Librarian, stated that access to services for disabled people in the community is an integral part of customer care, not separate from the rest of residents. A minimum of 3 per cent of library budgets has been spent on buying disability-related materials for loan and reference.

The National Library of Korea (NLK) is very committed to serving people with visual impairments using the Internet, and began digital library services in 2001. The NLK recognises that people who are visually impaired also have the same right as the rest of the population to gain access to publicly funded general libraries including school, university and public libraries. To reach this goal, the NLK is moving forward to the digital future. In 2003, the NLK began producing universities' textbook titles in digital format, and it has distributed them through its website to students with visual impairments from 2004. At the end of 2005, the NLK offered a total of 2,895 titles of textbooks used in 35 universities.

This web-based service reflects the NLK's commitment to integrate the visually impaired into the mainstream of library services by making its collections more useful and accessible. Before initiating this new service, the NLK, using the standard MAchine Readable Cataloging system (MARC), had already developed a union catalogue of alternative format materials, comprising 120,000 records that were housed by 32 libraries for students with visual impairments. These libraries have limited resources, and most of them are run by the private sector. Using the union catalogue to minimise duplicates helps them make the best use of their resources for alternative format materials. The union catalogue can be accessed via the KOLISNET, South Korean Library Information System Network (*www.nl.go. kr/kolisnet*), and also via a dedicated website at the NLK for visually impaired (*sigak.nl.go.kr/kn*).

In general, South Korea's government budget for people with disabilities to have access to information and to acquire IT equipment is equivalent to that of other areas. The South Korean government has recognised and is making every effort to decrease the digital divide between disadvantaged people, including people with disabilities, and those in society who have ready access to computers, the Internet and electronic information. One major step has been enacting the Act on Closing the Digital Divide in January 2001. The law mandated a Digital Divide Closure Master Plan, which was formulated in 2001. Following the plan, 13 government departments have implemented new projects to reduce digital gaps through funding, education and other initiatives.

The second phase of the five-year plan started in 2006 and to be completed in 2010, has resulted in South Korea investing 313 billion won (US$323 million) in 2006 on initiatives to promote universal access to electronic information. In addition, every year many new projects related to improving library services for people with disabilities have received funding from local/central government. For libraries in South Korea these days, it does not seem too difficult to secure financial resources to put a new idea for the disabled into action. Indeed, the problem faced by most libraries in South Korea is the shortage of staff with knowledge and experience in library services for people with disabilities.

Less prepared librarians and other stumbling blocks

As mentioned, discrimination has already become indisputably illegal in many countries. But human beings are motivated largely by self-interest. External factors are unlikely to change one's perception of a class of people, including people who have disabilities. Physical changes such as buildings, pavements, parking lots and lifts, can be easily mandated by law and carried out with money and a phone call. Law mandates rights, but cannot a mandate a positive attitude. Thus, changing attitudes can be a great challenge to librarians when they integrate people with disabilities into mainstream library services. Moreover, people normally do not like to change things that have previously worked well in their lives.

There are many stories of disabled people being discriminated against unintentionally in mainstream libraries. Much has been done by librarians who are insensitive or have limited experience and knowledge of the characteristics of disability and problems of disabled people. For instance, a man of this author's acquaintance once overheard a conversation between two librarians who were talking about him:

> 'That chap's sight is getting quite poor isn't it? He's always asking for help', said the first. His colleague responded, 'I think he can see a lot more than he admits. He dropped a pound coin earlier, he soon saw that and picked it up ... he can see when he wants to.'

Not surprisingly, the man has never been back to the library since that day. If the librarians in question had been more informed, they would have seen the fallacy of their own example. In his article, 'Understanding the problems of being partially sighted', Collins (1994) notes that if someone has lost their central vision, making it difficult for them to read and write, they may nevertheless be able to pinpoint a coin or other small shiny object on the floor, even at 4–5 metres, because it can be located through the peripheral vision as the head or eyes are moved.

Unfortunately, the aforementioned librarians failed to see the individual behind the disability. People with disabilities also are treated frequently as less intelligent than non-disabled people. As another example, a university staff member reported that a student with cerebral palsy, who had straight A grades in all of his class work, visited a number of libraries in the Washington area to secure archival material for a highly technical research paper. He felt that his requests were not being taken seriously and that visits to a number of related libraries yielded less information than they might have. Suspecting that those he had approached in person believed he could not possibly handle so complex a research problem, he sent typewritten requests in advance of future visits and was not surprised to find that the libraries in question indeed had a great deal of the material he sought.

From the point of view of people who have disabilities, psychological barriers are as daunting as physical and technical barriers. No barrier is more weighted than psychological barriers in mainstream settings for most disabled people. Sometimes physical and psychological barriers can be linked. For example, a library may believe that a ramp in the loading dock provides equal access. But if people in a wheelchair have to enter a library building through the route of delivered goods instead of the main entrance used by other people, this can cause a tremendous psychological barrier. In other cases, psychological barriers exist even when physical ones do not. These are mainly created by librarians' lack of knowledge of the characteristics of disabilities, a lack of interpersonal skills for working with people who have disabilities, and a negative attitude towards people who have disabilities.

Other examples of how non-disabled people's attitudes and behaviour influence the use of libraries by people with disabilities are numerous. A deaf student once remarked that she did not worry about her disability, but how she was treated by librarians would cause her great concern. She worried that they would regard her as stupid, treat her as a child, feel pity or regard her as a nuisance if she asked questions. Sometimes unwittingly, librarians can show the 'How many sugars does he take?' syndrome by treating disabled people as incapable clients, talking to interpreters, friends, or other third parties instead of talking directly to the patron. This kind of psychological barrier for disabled people to access library services creates one of the worst hindrances in using mainstream libraries. To remove these kinds of psychological barriers a new demand is being made on libraries to provide better staff training and education. This should be the most important issue in the integration of disabled people into mainstream library services.

The International Federation of Library Associations (IFLA) guidelines state that responsibility for the development, implementation, and operation of library services to clients with disabilities should be assigned to a professional librarian holding the degrees, certification and/or training pertaining to such professional status. Some libraries set up a department to address the needs of their patrons who have disabilities. In some libraries this approach works well. However, a special department can create more problems by its very existence. It goes against other principles of mainstream integration, and may tempt library management may to relegate disability services to the 'expert', effectively removing disability access issues from overall library service planning.

The example of Hwadojin Library in South Korea illustrates some of the problems of segregating disability services. There, the staff member who is in charge of disability-related services, is at a slightly lower level and does not take part in the decision-making at the highest level. This makes it difficult for disability services to be integrated into the library's overall planning, policy and budgets. To other staff members, this lack of top leadership commitment implies that disability services are not a true priority for the library. Even worse, because of the designation as a special library unit, the unit head has been frequently treated as an outsider among the other staff of the library. This makes the goal of mainstream integration especially difficult to achieve.

Instead, considering the library needs of people with disabilities should be driven from the top and involve all library staff. In the case of Islington Central Library in London, the designated person in charge of promoting better service is Principal of the library – who raises disability issues in every aspect of library services including the library's overall planning, policy and budgets. This top-level leadership demonstrates the library's commitment to improving services and helps build full staff commitment to reaching service goals.

In the user perspective, setting up a special unit for people with disabilities also could be an obstacle to library use. Paul Porter, a blind information officer at RNIB, who used to work for the Mitchell Library (a public library in Glasgow), has said that services or equipment for people with disabilities should not appear separated or different. When asked for his opinion about a special unit at a mainstream library for visually impaired people to use computers or to access electronic materials, he said that the unit should be integrated as part of the normal library set-up. Being separate or different is perceived as very negative in our society. People want to get the same treatment as everyone else.

Libraries who want to improve services surprisingly may face resistance from disability agencies or institutions themselves. Some of these institutions seem not to welcome integrating people with disabilities into the mainstream library services. In some cases, this may be due to concerns about people's opportunities. For example, some people fear that integrating children who are blind into mainstream schools may reduce their opportunity to become proficient Braille users. In other cases, the institutions may fear losing their share of scarce funding, or having a decrease in their institution's membership. In all cases, libraries should work closely with these agencies to build coalitions and displace fears.

Conclusion

The ultimate goal of integration is to help people who have disabilities use their abilities and develop their potential. This will only be done by providing all people with equal opportunities in all aspects of society. On an economic front, discriminating and excluding people who have disabilities from education, employment and social activities results in their having to live dependently and unproductively. The cost of lifelong support to disabled people is high and even wasteful. Money spent simply to maintain dependency is essentially lost.

Libraries can help reverse this situation. Building on legislative mandates and their own initiatives, they can create the physical and psychological environments needed to foster individual growth for people with disabilities. This will result in more people being able to realise their potential, to be financially independent, and to contribute the greatest benefit to society as a whole.

7

Low-cost/no-cost ways to improve service right now
Courtney Deines-Jones

Introduction

As evidenced by the other chapters of this book, there are numerous ways in which investments in adaptive technology, collections, equipment and facility modifications can pay great dividends to patrons who have disabilities. Librarians, library directors, trustees and service providers all should incorporate these whenever they are examining existing or proposed services.

In addition, librarians can do things right now – at little or no expense – to improve services. This chapter provides ideas for improving the library facility and providing the best service possible to all patrons. Participating in professional information exchanges such as those sponsored by IFLA[1] can help librarians identify even more ways to improve service. Librarians are strongly encouraged to do whatever they can, whenever they can. Even the smallest step can make a very large difference.

Barriers to library use

Some libraries are frequented by few patrons who have disabilities. In my consulting experience, I have found that many librarians conclude from this that there must not be any such people in the community, or that people with disabilities do not want to use the library. This simply is false. People with disabilities have information needs. They enjoy recreational reading. They want their children to benefit from story hours and enrichment programmes. There are barriers, however, that can stop people with disabilities from wanting to use the library. Some common barriers are:

- *Assuming there is nothing 'for us' in the library*: Many potential patrons still believe that the library offers only traditional print materials. If they cannot use traditional print format, these people will see no reason to visit or use the library's services.

- *Identifying the library as a government institution*: Many people with disabilities have difficulty getting the support and services they need from the government. Some may have been victims of arcane institutional systems and bureaucracies. These potential patrons may assume that using the library will be a similarly negative experience.

- *Being uncertain that librarians will be able to communicate*: People who communicate through sign language, Braille, or other non-verbal/non-print means may assume that librarians will not be able to understand them.

- *Having negative past experiences*: Unfortunately, people with disabilities do face discrimination, sometimes at the hands of librarians. It only takes one negative experience to make a person reluctant to visit the library again. Someone who was treated unfairly as a child may not revisit the library again for the rest of his or her life.

Involving the community

A first step to removing these barriers and improving service is to reach out beyond the library walls and into the community. This can be done by talking with people, encouraging them to visit the library, and providing information about the materials and services people can use. It also can take the form of presenting actual programmes such as storytime sessions and services such as book delivery to institutions at schools, community centres and similar locales. People from the community also can be engaged to help with service planning and improvement tasks such as:

- identifying needs of current and potential patrons with specific disabilities;

- serving as speakers and trainers to help build staff awareness;

- reviewing library services and facilities to suggest ways to improve service;

- acting as a bridge to the community to help build familiarity among potential patrons of what the library has to offer.

Potential community outreach sources can include both disability-specific and general community organisations. These include non-government organisations, advocacy groups, schools, faith-based organisations, senior citizens' councils and community groups.

Librarians should make every effort to include leaders of communities of people who have disabilities in library service planning and as advocates for better library services. Service improvements will be most effective when they are designed to meet the real needs of real people. As demand for such services grows and the number of people with disabilities using the library increases, librarians will have justification to further increase resources and make even more improvements. The result can be a self-sustaining model of service excellence.

Listservs and professional exchanges can be very powerful tools to improve service. As an example, an exchange over the SLB listserv in autumn 2006 involved a librarian with a young patron in Somaliland who desperately wanted to learn Braille despite having lost his hands in a landmine explosion. Through the listserv, the librarian received suggestions for high and low-tech solutions from all over the world. He was able to reach other librarians (notably in Vietnam) who had faced the same challenge, and ultimately had several potential strategies to help the boy realise his dream of reading.

Improving the physical facility

Often, librarians do not try to offer services to people with disabilities because they believe their facilities are inaccessible. Even when this is true, improvements to the library space can be made at little or no cost. The requirements are only that librarians and library staff know their libraries and remain conscious of the needs of all their patrons. The following sections offer some 'quick fixes' for librarians working in libraries that are not fully accessible.

Facilitating movement through the library

People who have mobility impairments or visual disabilities will find moving through the library much easier if aisles are clean, signs are clear, and guidance is given. Librarians should survey their physical facility to answer several questions.

- *Can someone open the door?* People with limited physical strength may have difficulty opening doors that require more than about 2.27 kg (5 pounds) of force. If the door is hard to open, install a doorbell or other signalling device with a sign that instructs patrons to ring for assistance. Remember that interior doors may also be hard to open. If it is appropriate, prop open such doors to facilitate movement within the library. If the doors must be closed, be sensitive to their location so that you can proactively offer to assist people travelling through the library.

- *Can someone with a wheelchair navigate the area?* Librarians should know where there are stairs, broken ground or flooring, or other obvious barriers. An easy way to determine whether someone using a wheelchair can get around furniture or browse stacks of books is to take a metre-long ruler or stick, hold it perpendicular to one's body, and physically walk through the library. Wherever you can walk without the stick touching, a person using a wheelchair will be able to move forward. To turn around comfortably or pass someone else using a wheelchair, the person will need a space of about two sticks. Librarians should note which areas are not accessible and what is stored there so that they do not needlessly send patrons off to inaccessible sections of the library.

- *Is there adequate headroom?* Headroom is most commonly problematic in transitional areas such as doorways and stairs, especially in older buildings. Tall, visually impaired people face the most danger from these obstacles. Other transient headroom problems may be caused by banners, displays or hanging plants that are hung from the ceiling. Even when such a barrier will not cause injury, it can give someone quite a fright to suddenly feel something against their head when they are expecting to be navigating a clear walkway. The general rule is to hang things so that they reach no lower than two metres above the floor. If you have a tall patron base, you may want to increase this somewhat. Librarians should clearly mark any hazardous low spots.

- *Are there trip hazards or other possible barriers?* Common barriers include single steps that are hard to see; stairs that are uneven, non-rectangular (as with circular staircases), or of an unusual rise/run ratio; highly contrasting floor tiles that may look like changes in elevation to people with visual impairments; area rugs, protective floor coverings and transitions from hard floors to carpeted areas; and clutter blocking walkways, aisles and public areas. Librarians should eliminate these when possible, mark them clearly if it is not, and be ready to offer assistance when they know a patron will find navigation difficult or impossible.

Making spaces more inviting

In addition to being accessible, spaces should be inviting. This is especially true for people who use wheelchairs, walkers and other mobility aids. The following suggestions can help you make your facility more welcoming. Figure 7.1 provides a facility checklist you can use on a daily basis to be sure the library is as inviting as possible.[2]

- *Keep accessible counter space free of clutter.* If you have a low counter space at the reference or circulation desk, keep it clear. People who use wheelchairs should be able to use these spaces to conduct business.

Figure 7.1   Daily facility checklist

Daily facility walk-through

Check each area of your department or branch to ensure walkways are clear and there are no obstructions to access by people with disabilities. Note any problems you cannot correct and bring them to the attention of your supervisor.

	Item
	Doorways are clear and doors open easily
	Floors are dry, carpet is flat, edges of rain/snow mats are flush with the floor
	Floors and work areas are clear of trash and debris
	Book trucks, step stools, plants, displays, etc. do not block accessible routes, facilities or areas
	Wheelchair accessible areas are not blocked by chairs or other furniture
	Signage is clear, accurate, and visible
	Banners and displays hang no lower than two metres from the floor where people walk
	Items (such as plants and displays) do not extend into accessible routes
	Accessible workstations and adaptive equipment are working
	Adaptive equipment held in storage (for example, magnifiers or listening devices) are in place and accounted for
	Hazardous areas such as uneven or wet floors are marked from all accessible sides
	Signage is in place to advise patrons of any temporarily inaccessible areas

Please describe any other access concerns:

_____

_____

_____

- *Maintain empty spaces at study tables and reading areas*: Each study and reading area should have at least one space left open at a table, one study carrel without a chair pulled up to the desk, and 'empty' space in the lounge or reading room seating area. This makes it clear that people who use wheelchairs are welcome in all parts of the library.

- *Avoid setting up 'special' areas*: Librarians should make every effort to encourage library patrons to use all appropriate public areas. This means placing equipment and maintaining study space for people who have disabilities throughout the library. In some cases, as with collections of audio materials, it may make sense to house certain types of materials and equipment together. Even when this is true, however, patrons should be made to feel welcome in whatever section of the library they choose to use.

  Accessible is not always inviting. As an example, a university library I once visited was keen to be sure a study space was available for people with disabilities – so they left a spot free and glued a very large, bright blue international accessibility sticker to the table. The librarian I talked with seemed genuinely mystified that students using mobility aids did not want to sit at the spot marked with the big blue wheelchair. Patrons want to have access. They also want to feel welcome *everywhere*, not just at the spot with the big blue sign.

Making it easier for people to see and hear

With some simple improvements, librarians can make it easier for their patrons to see and hear them. This will improve communications and make the library experience more enjoyable for both patrons and staff.

- *Provide proper lighting*: Lights at circulation and reference desks should be placed so that people's faces are clearly illuminated and not in shadow. Work areas should be well lit. Computers should be positioned to eliminate glare, or should be provided with glare screens. Better lighting can make it easier to communicate with people who have hearing impairments or read lips. It also helps people who have visual impairments read materials more easily.

- *Use clearly printed signage*: When making temporary signs for library spaces or events, use clear writing and high-contrast colours for paper and ink. Directional signs should have simple, bold characters that are at least 5–10 cm high whenever possible.

- *Test announcement systems*: People working at libraries with public address systems should routinely listen to how loud and clear they are in all sections of the library. If voices seem soft or unclear in some areas, librarians can personally announce things (e.g. 'the library will be closing in 15 minutes') to patrons in those sections.

- *Be sensitive when making print materials*: When developing handouts and bibliographic aids, use the largest font practical (16 point or larger is ideal) and use dark characters on a light coloured paper. Librarians who have access to a scanner or enlarging copier can reproduce standard print materials in an enlarged format for distribution to people with reduced vision.

Making it easier for people to find things

In addition to removing barriers and noting those that cannot be removed, librarians can facilitate navigation through their space. When patrons can find what they need easily and independently, they are more likely to want to visit the library. Common-sense signage and communication can improve independent navigation by library users. These will benefit all patrons, not only those who have disabilities.

- *Put signs up consistently*: Good signage is key to finding spaces. Signs should indicate all major areas of the library, accessible paths of travel, accessible toilets and other facilities, areas that are not accessible, and places patrons can go for assistance. Signs should be placed consistently, especially where Braille is used, so that people know where to find them.

- *Be sure signs are not obstructed*: Potted plants, easels, displays and the like should be arranged so that they do not block signs.

- *Provide straight lines of travel*: Do not put temporary signs or displays in the middle of a travel path.

- *Provide maps, including in large print and tactile formats*: Maps should indicate major areas of the library, accessible paths of travel, emergency exits, accessible toilets and other facilities, areas that are not accessible, and places patrons can go for assistance. Librarians with access to computers or enlarging copiers should make a supply of large format maps for use by people with visual impairments.

  Making a map may seem silly in a tiny library, but some people find remembering locations even in a small area very difficult. Having a map saves the patron from having to repeatedly ask where certain things are. It also helps when explaining collection locations to people who do not communicate orally or who have difficulty understanding or remembering spoken directions. Even a one-room library can benefit from a simple map showing doors, basic facilities and collection locations.

Tactile maps also can be made for use by people who are blind, even for people who do not have access to wax printers or similar printing tools. Some innovative ways of making such maps that I have seen include tracing print maps using puffy paint, gluing string over the lines of a print map, and having a woodwork class build a tactile scale model of a school library as a project.

- *Let patrons know of any changes to the library*: Librarians should inform patrons when they are anticipating changes to the layout of the facility or location of collections and equipment. Signs should explain when the change is to take place, and where patrons will be able to find the materials or services they need once the change is in process or complete. After the move or reorganisation is complete and until new permanent signs are made, temporary signs should be made and prominently displayed.

  Let patrons know of any changes to materials locations. Occasionally, cataloguing rule changes may lead to reclassification and consequent relocation of library materials. Librarians also sometimes move segments of the collection (such as to a local collection, or for a special seasonal display). When this happens, librarians should put signs up in the 'old' location indicating where the materials can be found.

Improving service

Improving service can be done by increasing awareness, improving attitudes about serving people with disabilities, and training staff. Service improvement strategies often cost very little, and will greatly benefit both patrons and staff.

Addressing staff attitudes

Staff may give adequate service as a part of their job duties, but they will provide excellent service only if they want to. In my work with librarians, I have found that most negative attitudes hindering service can be traced back to three main fears: that the person with a disability may present a threat to the worker's health or safety; that the person with a disability will take a lot of time to help; and that the staff member will not know how to help the person with the disability. Additionally, some cultures attach serious negative connotations to disability, or to certain disabilities.

Training courses with ongoing participation from community members can help overcome these fears. In addition, librarians can do things right away that will help staff improve their attitudes toward serving all patrons.

- *Understand attitudinal barriers*: Each staff member's own experiences will inform how they approach service to people with disabilities. If they have had positive personal encounters with a broad range of people, they likely will be more receptive to strategies for improving library services. Staff members who have had little contact or whose contact has been negative similarly may be more reluctant. A sample attitudinal survey is found in Figure 7.2.[3]

- *Introduce members of the community*: When library staff get to know people who have disabilities, they will be more comfortable helping them. Community members can explain what they need to be able to use the library – what formats they prefer, how they like to look for information, and how library staff can most effectively communicate with them. If possible, hire people with disabilities and recruit them as volunteers to work throughout the library.

Figure 7.2 Sample staff attitudinal survey

In our ongoing effort to improve library services to all patrons, the library is soliciting your ideas for training and awareness programmes. Please think about your work with library users who have disabilities – what worked, what didn't, and where you think training would help you and your peers perform your job better.

Please rate how much you agree with the following statements on a 1–5 scale. A rating of '1' means you don't agree at all; a rating of '5' means you agree completely.

I am very confident helping library patrons who use wheelchairs or have other mobility impairments.	1	2	3	4	5
I am very confident helping library users who are blind or have visual impairments.	1	2	3	4	5
I am very confident helping library users who are deaf or have hearing loss.	1	2	3	4	5
I am very confident helping library users who have mental disabilities.	1	2	3	4	5
I understand the library's policies and how they apply to providing service to our patrons who have disabilities.	1	2	3	4	5
I am familiar with the library's adaptive technology and know how to use it.	1	2	3	4	5
Serving people who have disabilities is a daily part of my job.	1	2	3	4	5
Serving people with disabilities would create a lot of problems for me.	1	2	3	4	5
Our library currently does an excellent job serving people who have disabilities	1	2	3	4	5

If you could attend two courses designed to improve your ability to help library users who have disabilities, what topics would they cover?

1. _____

2. _____

Please describe any other ideas or suggestions about how the library can improve our services to patrons with disabilities:

_____

_____

_____

- *Realistically explain disabilities*: When working with American public libraries in the early 1990s, I encountered many people who would wear gloves when helping people whom they thought were HIV-positive. Despite the overwhelming evidence to the contrary, they were afraid of 'catching' AIDS. On the other hand, some of these same librarians had no problem working unprotected and in close quarters with people sick with colds or flu.

  Staff must be informed about outbreaks and disabling conditions (such as tuberculosis) that indeed may be contagious and told how to protect themselves. They also should be explicitly told how disabling conditions occur to dispel myths.

- *Ensure policies are fair and that library staff understand how to enforce them*: Library staff need to understand what policies govern library use and behaviour and what is to be done if people violate those policies. For example, if a library tolerates crying babies or loud children, it should also tolerate adults who inappropriately vocalise. At the same time, library staff need to know what to do when a patron is abusive, threatening, destructive, or otherwise presents a threat, regardless of whether the patron has a disability.

- *Provide training for all staff members on adaptive equipment and features*: Expanding the pool of people who can help someone will immediately help people. Just as libraries conduct regular fire drills, it is important to keep people's skills up to date. If you have adaptive equipment, computer software, or other tools to help people access information, be sure every staff member understands how to use it. Have refresher training at least quarterly, especially if the equipment is used only occasionally.

Making all patrons feel welcome

Library staff may be reluctant to greet patrons with disabilities because they would rather say nothing at all than say the wrong thing. Understanding simple etiquette can help alleviate staff fears and help make all patrons feel welcome.

- *Make eye contact when you greet patrons*: Making eye contact shows you are directly interested in a patron. If the library user is deaf, he or she will be able to see that you are speaking and can respond. Library users with reduced vision will hear your greeting and may have sufficient vision to be able to see and understand your facial expression.

- *Accept 'no' for an answer*: Sometimes patrons want to use the library independently. If a patron declines your offer for help, honour their request. If you are sure your greeting or offer of help has been understood and a patron still ignores you, let it go. People may ignore greetings for any number of reasons.

- *Talk directly to the patron*: A patron may come to the library with an interpreter, may speak using a communications board or similar tool, or may have an assistant. In all cases, library staff should face and talk directly to the patron. This is a matter of basic respect and reinforces the understanding that it is the patron him or herself who is receiving service.

- *Keep paper and pencil on hand*: Even if your staff are fluent in sign language, some patrons who are deaf or have hearing impairments may not be. Writing things down may be the most effective way to be sure the patron's need is properly understood and that the patron gets what he or she wants. Keeping ready a pencil and paper of a reasonable size to write notes on also makes it easy to write down instructions, references, or other information.

- *Remain at eye level for extended transactions*: Whenever possible, put yourself at the patron's eye level when engaging in extended reference interviews or other transactions. Pull up a chair for yourself, or sit at a desk or table. Similarly, when walking with a person who uses a mobility aid, walk alongside the patron whenever possible so that you can see each other during conversation.

- *Avoid 'diminutive' forms of address*: Terms like 'sweetie' or 'dear' imply that the person being spoken to is at the intellectual level of a child. No matter the intent, they are not appropriate in a professional setting. People with disabilities – including those with intellectual impairments – should be addressed in the same manner as their non-disabled peers as a matter of common courtesy and respect.

- *Accommodate service animals*: While service dogs are most commonly associated with people who are blind, many people with disabilities use a broad variety of service animals. Traditionally, service animals are dogs, but many animals may be used as aides. The Guide Horse Foundation (*www.guidehorse.org*) is a US organisation providing miniature horses to assist people with disabilities. Service animals should be allowed into libraries.

- *Volunteer information on equipment and services*: Patrons may not know about tools your library has. If you are helping a patron who might benefit from adaptive technology, ask if it would be helpful. For example, if you are helping someone who seems to have trouble reading standard print, let the patron know about screen readers, magnifiers, CCTV aids, hand-held magnifying glasses or other equipment you have on hand. Offer to show patrons how to use the tools and stay with them until you are sure they understand how the equipment works.

Helping people who have specific disabilities

All of the techniques listed above are applicable to every library user, regardless of their disability status. There are also ways to better serve people with specific disabilities.

Blindness and visual disabilities

■ Provide specific, detailed instructions that include approximate distances. Describe the location of stairs, changes in terrain, or other obstacles as precisely as possible. Explain where Braille signs or controls are located. For example, say 'To get to the music room, go ahead about 5 metres until this corridor ends and turn left. The room is about 30 metres straight ahead and is on the right-hand side just after you reach a carpeted area. There is a Braille sign to the right of the door.'

■ When helping blind library users, identify yourself and ask if the patron needs assistance. If you are in a conversation and someone else joins, announce that person's arrival and departure.

■ If you are guiding a blind patron, offer your elbow and lead by it. Announce upcoming turns, obstacles such as doors or stairs, and whether you will be going up or down the stairs or ramps.

- Do not automatically assume a patron who uses a cane is totally blind. Many people with visual impairments and some with other disabilities use a cane both as a navigational aid and as a clue to others that they may not respond to audible or visual cues.

- Ask what information the patron needs and what formats he or she prefers. Each user is an individual – one may prefer large print where another prefers digital talking books.

Deafness and hearing impairments

- Speak directly to the patron, not to an interpreter. If you are using a telephone or telephone/Internet relay service, understand that everything you say will be repeated verbatim to the patron, including side comments or conversations. For example, if you say 'tell him we don't have that book', the interpreter will repeat you exactly. He or she will *not* say 'they don't have that book'.

- Speak in a normal tone of voice. Shouting or exaggerating enunciation does not help people who have hearing loss. It also distorts the mouth so that lip readers have a more difficult time understanding.

- Write down information using generously sized paper, not small scraps. Bring paper and pen or pencil with you when you are escorting people so that questions can be asked and answered as they arise.

- If possible, learn basic sign language and practise it with colleagues. While not all people who are deaf use sign language, many do. Learning sign is the equivalent of learning a second verbal language to accommodate a multicultural clientele.

- To get the attention of someone who is deaf, position yourself in their line of sight. If they are studying or sleeping, try gently tapping on the desk or counter while standing in front of them. Always stay in front of the person, in their line of sight. Do not tap someone on the shoulder or otherwise touch a patron unexpectedly or without permission.

- If your library does not have a strobe or other visible announcement system, be sure to have someone physically walk through the library if there is a fire alarm or to announce that the library will be closing. Operate under the assumption that someone in the building may not be able to hear the alarm or announcement.

Mobility impairments

- Ask if patrons need assistance. If a patron requests information you know to be on an inaccessible (too high or too low) shelf, go with the patron. Page the books or material and arrange them at an accessible workstation, or put them on a sturdy, non-tippable book truck for the patron to browse independently.

- If a patron requests information that is in an inaccessible location, say so and offer to bring the books or material to the patron. If the patron does not know exactly what he or she wanted, facilitate browsing by bringing down a book truck with general materials from the area.

- Remember that mobility impairments can affect more than the ability to walk or to reach tall shelves. Some people may have difficulty stooping. Others may have limited arm strength or a restricted range of motion.

Learning disabilities

- Some people better understand information that is presented graphically. Providing a map of the library with the location of things the patron needs clearly indicated may be more effective than giving directions aloud or in writing.

- Focus on the exact needs of the patron. For example, do not start teaching Internet browsing skills to a patron who needs to locate one specific book.

- Keep language clear and concise.

- Speak clearly using a normal tone of voice. Shouting, speaking excessively slowly, or using an unnaturally high-pitched voice does not improve comprehension.

- Encourage people to ask for help and show them where the nearest staffed help desks are. Stay with patrons until you are sure they understand how to find the information they want and how to get additional assistance if it is needed.

Low-cost tools and equipment

The following low-cost tools and equipment that may help your library serve more people better. Some are designed for use by people with disabilities; others are general tools that fill this purpose.

- *Accessibility options for computers*: Options built into Windows and Macintosh operating systems allow people to adjust display magnification, colour schemes, and other options. These are free and in Windows can be activated from the control panel. Librarians should understand what options are available, and should be able to activate accessibility options without calling tech support.

- *Bed risers*: These are plastic cups designed to raise beds several inches off the floor and can be used to raise tables or study carrels if needed to accommodate people who use wheelchairs. They are sturdy and can be installed or removed without hardware. Library staff should check to be sure the resulting table height is approximately 70–85 cm from the ground, with at least 70 cm of leg room underneath.

- *Chopsticks*: Chopsticks can extend a person's reach while using kiosks, touch screens, or any equipment with easy-to-press buttons. They are better than pencils for this use because there is no 'lead end', which can leave a mess and can be too pointy to work effectively on some screens.

- *Cookbook stand*: Cookbook stands help people who have a hard time holding a book or holding it open. They are most appropriate for uses where frequent page-turns are not required.

- *Copy stand*: Copy stands help keep information secure and easily visible. They are especially useful for people with limited range of motion.

- *Doorbell (battery operated)*: Placed at interior and exterior doors, doorbells allow patrons to alert the librarian that assistance is needed.

- *Duct tape*: Duct tape is ugly but very useful, inside and out. It can secure curling mats to the floor and cover dangerous cords and similar trip hazards. Duct tape is available in bright colours that can be used to draw attention to hazardous areas.

- *Grabber/reach extender*: These tools are useful for retrieving paperbacks, unbound magazines, or light books, or for picking things up from the floor. They should not be used to retrieve heavy books from high shelves.

- *Lamp (battery operated)*: A small, portable battery-operated lamp can be used in any area where lighting is poor. Battery operated laps are suggested because they do not have to be used near an outlet and they do not have cords, which can be a trip hazard.

- *Magnifier (sheet or hand-held)*: While not as versatile as CCTV magnifiers, hand-held magnifiers can help people with reduced vision read standard or small-print text.

- *Pattern weights*: These plastic-coated lead weights are designed for use on patterns for sewing. They can be used to hold open larger books or to hold maps and large documents in place.

- *Periscope*: Inexpensive plastic periscopes with shatterproof mirrors can be used to allow people with limited range of motion to browse high or low shelves independently.

- *Puffy fabric paint*: Puffy paint comes in a number of colours and can be used to make tactile maps.

- *Online tools*: Libraries with Internet access can provide their patrons with immediate access to a wealth of information, resources and online tools specifically for people with disabilities.

- *Resource notebook*: A one-stop compilation of resources available to people with disabilities is useful for staff and patrons alike.

- *Rubber bands*: Provide greater grip strength for opening microfiche and similar containers.

- *Step stool*: Sturdy step stools are handy for reaching tall shelves without having to reach overhead or bring heavy books down from a dangerous height.

Conclusion

Libraries should be designed to be universally accessible, and should have equipment in place to enable all users to get the maximum benefit of the library's material and service offerings. Even when this is not possible, however, library workers have the means to improve their facilities and services for use by patrons who have disabilities. This chapter has presented some ideas. In addition to exploring them, staff, patrons and community members who have disabilities should be asked for their suggestions for things that can make library use a little easier.

Notes

1. IFLA, the Section for Libraries Serving Disadvantaged Persons, and the Section for Libraries for the Blind (SLB) each offer listservs allowing members to broadcast news, requests for help, and other information.
2. Adapted from Deines-Jones and Van Fleet (1995).
3. Adapted from Deines-Jones (1999).

8

Further reading and resources
Laura Roberts Gottlieb

Introduction

Since the passage of the Americans with Disability Act 1990, much has been published on library service to patrons with disabilities. The resources detailed in this chapter have been selected to provide an introduction and practical guide to improving service in a range of settings. The list is by no means exhaustive, however, the bibliographies contained in these sources would be a good guide for those wishing to delve more deeply into any topic.

This chapter is divided into several sections. The first section is a brief annotated bibliography of books, articles and websites that provide information on library service to people with disabilities. The second section lists several different guidelines for library accessibility. Next is a list of organisations for people with disabilities, many of which have additional information on their websites. The final section suggests some resources for securing funding to increase access for all patrons.

Bibliography

- Abledata, available at: *http://www.abledata.com*

An assistive technology site sponsored by the National Institute on Disability and Rehabilitation Research, part of the US Department of Education. It includes objective information on a wide variety of assistive devices, as well as references to general information on disabilities, governmental resources and research.

■ Agada, J. and Dauenheimer, D. (2001) 'Beyond ADA: crossing borders to understand the psychosocial needs of students with disabilities', in H. A. Thomson (ed.) *Crossing the Divide: Proceedings of the Tenth National Conference of the Association of College and Research Libraries*, Chicago: American Library Association; pp. 295–302.

Agada and Dauenheimer show the importance of moving beyond physical access to libraries and addressing the social and emotional factors that also impede access. The article includes several helpful scenarios that illustrate why persons with disabilities might feel uncomfortable in the library and what library staff can do to improve the situation.

■ Deines-Jones, C. and Van Fleet, C. (1995) *Preparing Staff to Serve Patrons with Disabilities*, New York: Neal-Schuman Publishers, Inc.

Focusing on day-to-day operations, this work provides a ready reference on library services to people with disabilities. Organised by service areas, it includes common problem scenarios and solutions as well as reproducible forms and checklists.

■ Forrest, M. E. S. (2006) 'Toward an accessible academic library: using the *IFLA Checklist*', *IFLA Journal* 32(1): 13–18.

Forrest describes and analyses the experience of applying the *IFLA Checklist, Access to Libraries for Persons with*

Disabilities to an academic library in the UK. The article also includes an introduction to disability legislation in the UK.

- Hernon, P. and Calvert, P. (eds) (2006) *Improving the Quality of Library Services for Students with Disabilities*, Westport, CN: Libraries Unlimited.

This book presents a model that applies quality assessment to programmes for students with disabilities in academic libraries. The first seven chapters provide a nice overview of services at a range of academic libraries in the USA and New Zealand.

- Laurent Clerc National Deaf Education Center (2006) 'Information on deafness', available at: *http://clerccenter .gallaudet.edu/infotogo/*

Affiliated with Gallaudet University, the Clerc Center provides a centralised source of information relating to deaf and hard of hearing children and adults. The site is organised by topic and is also searchable. Topics include communication, education, parenting, organisations and services/programmes for deaf individuals.

- Peters, T. and Bell, L. (2006) 'Hello IM, Goodbye TTY', *Computers in Libraries* 26(5): 18–21.

The article offers ideas for providing effective library service for the hearing impaired. It focuses on technologies in use, with an eye toward newer technologies, including instant messaging.

- Mates, B. T. (2004) 'Information access for people with disabilities', *Library Technology Reports* 40(3): 10–33.

This is a helpful guide to increasing computer access for patrons with disabilities. It features a summary of adaptive technologies available for people with visual impairments, learning disabilities, mobility impairments, cognitive difficulties and hearing impairments.

- Oliver, K. (1997) 'The spirit of the law: when ADA compliance means overall excellence in service to patrons with disabilities', *Public Libraries* 36(5): 294–8.

Oliver showcases how the Johnson County (Kansas) Library system addressed the challenges posed by the Americans with Disabilities Act. It provides a nice model for libraries confronting this issue for the first time or trying to improve access.

- Pollitt, C. and van Bodengraven, M. (2003) 'Making websites and OPACs accessible', *IFLA Journal* 29(4): 357–63.

Pollitt and van Bodengraven explain the importance of World Wide Web and online catalogue accessibility for visually-handicapped users. They explain how to increase accessibility and offer several examples from the European Union.

- Robertson, G. (2004) '"It's not just the books!" Wheelchair patrons speak out', *Feliciter* 50(6): 258–60.

This article provides a positive look at how libraries can be a 'safe spot' for patrons with disabilities. Those interviewed praise librarians' patience, awareness of potential problems and willingness to help.

- Roos, J. W. (2005) 'Copyright protection as an access barrier for those who read differently: the case for an international approach', *IFLA Journal* 31(1): 52–67.

This article discusses access barriers to print posed by copyright protection, possible solutions and lessons learned so far. Roos also includes a summary of the legal position in the USA, Canada, Australia and the European Union.

■ Rubin, R. J. (2001) *Planning for Library Services to People with Disabilities*, Chicago: Association of Specialized and Cooperative Library Agencies, American Library Association.

This book provides a nuts-and-bolts guide to preparing a plan to improve service to people with disabilities. It includes reproducible worksheets, questionnaires and tip sheets on communicating with people with disabilities. The book also contains a helpful glossary and bibliographies.

■ Solomon, A. (1994) 'Defiantly deaf', *The New York Times Magazine*, 28 August, p. 38.

This engaging article provides a window into American deaf culture and emphasises the similarities and differences within the group.

■ Taylor, J. M. (2004) 'Serving blind readers in a digital age', *American Libraries* 34(11): 49–51.

Taylor provides a brief summary of the history of the National Library Service for the Blind and Physically Handicapped's talking-book programme and a look toward the future of the digital book programme they will implement in 2008.

■ Tucker, R. N. (2003) 'Access for all? It depends on who you are', *IFLA Journal* 29(4): 385–8.

Tucker makes a strong argument for the needs of visually-impaired patrons in the developing world.

■ Turner, R. (1996) *Library Patrons with Disabilities*, San Antonio, TX: White Buffalo Press.

Turner offers a practical look at service to patrons with disabilities. The book includes many suggestions for improving physical access to information and library services as well as a chapter on why patrons with disabilities use the library.

- Wright, K. C. and Davie, J. F. (1989) *Library and Information Services for Handicapped Individuals, Third Edition*, Englewood, CO: Libraries Unlimited.

This is a good overview of library service to people with disabilities. It includes chapters on myths and stereotypes, legal issues, blind and visually impaired, deaf and hearing impaired, speech handicapped, mentally handicapped, physically handicapped, aging, and individuals with contagious diseases (specifically AIDS). Each chapter also includes suggestions for staff development activities to increase understanding of individuals with disabilities and evaluate library service to these individuals.

- Wright, K. C. and Davie, J. F. (1990) *Library Manager's Guide to Hiring and Serving Disabled Persons*. Jefferson, NC: McFarland and Company.

This book focuses on systemic aspects of the library, rather than public services, that affect disabled persons' access to the library. There are chapters on staff development, recruiting and hiring, selection and acquisition of materials, organisation of the collection, facility accessibility, public service programmes and information services.

- Velleman, R. A. (1990) *Meeting the Needs of People with Disabilities: A Guide for Librarians, Educators, and other Service Professionals*, Phoenix, AZ: Oryx Press.

This useful handbook is organised into four parts: an overview, consumer information, rehabilitation and special education, and library applications. It includes succinct definitions of many disabilities as well as easily-accessed resources on each topic.

- W3C (2006) *Web Accessibility Initiative*, available at: *http://www.w3.org/wai/*

W3C is an international consortium that develops web standards and guidelines. Their Web Accessibility Initiative guidelines are widely regarded as the international standard for web accessibility. Available on the website are the guidelines themselves (referenced below) and the draft of the next version of the guidelines, along with support and reference materials on web accessibility.

- Walling, L. Lucas and Karrenbrock, M. H. (1993) *Disabilities, Children, and Libraries: Mainstreaming Services in Public Libraries and School Library Media Centers.* Englewood, CO: Libraries Unlimited, Inc.

Although this book focuses on children's services, much of its information is equally applicable for all groups of library patrons. It covers a range of disabilities and how they affect patrons' use of the library as well as issues related to programming, selecting materials and adaptive technology. The chapter on sources is an excellent guide to US resources for children and adults.

- WebXACT, available at: *http://webxact.watchfire.com*

Formerly known as Bobby, this online service tests websites for accessibility issues such as alternative text, colour, tables and links. The initial review is free, and the service can do a more in-depth analysis for a fee. The site and results can be a bit confusing, but it provides a good quick check of your website's accessibility and highlights any problems.

- Zipkowitz, F. (ed.) (1996) *Reference Services for the Unserved*, Binghamton, NY: The Haworth Press.

A reprint of *The Reference Librarian* Number 53, 1996, this brief edited volume explores services to patrons with mental illness, disabled students and battered women. An annotated bibliography lists a number of resources on access for people of underserved cultural groups and in an international setting.

Guidelines and standards for serving patrons with disabilities

- Association of Specialized and Cooperative Library Agencies (2005) *Revised Standards and Guidelines of Service for the Library of Congress Network of Libraries for the Blind and Physically Handicapped*, Chicago: American Library Association.

- Association of Specialized and Cooperative Library Agencies (1996) *Guidelines for Library and Information Services for the American Deaf Community*, Chicago: American Library Association.

- Irvall, B. and Nielson, G. S. (2005) *IFLA Checklist: Access to Libraries for Persons with Disabilities*, IFLA Professional Reports No. 89, International Federation of Library Associations and Institutions, available at: *http://www.ifla.org/VII/s9/nd1/iflapr-89e.pdf*

- Day, J. M. (2000) *Guidelines for Library Services to Deaf People* (2nd edn) IFLA Professional Reports No. 62, International Federation of Library Associations and Institutions, available at: *http://www.ifla.org/VII/s9/nd1/iflapr-62e.pdf*

- Kavanaugh, R. and Skold, B. C, (2005) *Libraries for the Blind in the Information Age: Guidelines for Development*, IFLA Professional Reports No. 86, International Federation of Library Associations and

Institutions, available at *http://www.ifla.org/VII/s31/ pub/Profrep86.pdf*

■ Web Content Accessibility Working Group (1999) *Web Content Accessibility Guidelines 1.0*, available at: *http:// www.w3.org/TR/WCAG10/*

Organisations

■ American Library Association: Association of Specialized and Cooperative Library Agencies, 50 E. Huron Street, Chicago, IL 60611, USA; Tel: +1 312 280 4398; *http:// www.ala.org/ala/ascla/ascla.htm*

■ Disabled Peoples' International, 902–388 Portage Avenue, Winnipeg, Manitoba, R3C 0C8, Canada: Tel: +1 204 287 8010; Fax: +1 204 783 6270; *http://www. dpi.org*

■ IFLA: Libraries Serving Disadvantaged Persons Section, PO Box 95312, 2509 CH The Hague, Netherlands; Tel: +31 70 3140884; Fax: +31 70 3834827; *http://www.ifla .org/VII/s9/index.htm*

■ IFLA: Libraries for the Blind Section, PO Box 95312, 2509 CH The Hague, Netherlands; Tel: +31 70 3140884; Fax: +31 70 3834827; *http://www.ifla.org/VII/s31/ index.htm*

■ The National Library Service for the Blind and Physically Handicapped, The Library of Congress, Washington, DC 20542, USA; Tel: +1 202 707-5000 *http://www.loc .gov/nls*

■ World Federation of the Deaf, PO Box 65, FIN-00401, Helsinki, Finland; Fax: +358 9 580 3572; *http://www .wfdeaf.org*

■ Rehabilitation International, RI Secretariat, 25 East 21 Street, 4th floor, New York, NY 10010, USA; Tel: +1 212 420 1500; Fax: +1 212 505 0871; *http://www.rehab-international.org/*

Funding

Resources for finding grants

■ The Foundation Center, 79 Fifth Avenue/16th Street, New York, NY 10003-3076; Tel: +1 212 620 4230; Fax: +1 212 807 3677; *www.foundationcenter.org*

Established in 1956, The Foundation Center maintains a comprehensive database of US grantmakers and their grants. Their website has a section specifically for disability resources, a searchable database of foundations, a listing of current requests for proposals, and tutorials on completing applications and proposals. While there is a fee for their online database, they also offer Cooperating Collections, a core collection of their materials available at libraries around the country. Notably, the Cooperating Collections include their *Guide to Funding for International and Foreign Programs*. The website's section for international visitors (*http://foundationcenter.org/getstarted/ international/*) links to additional information on international grantmaking, including a bibliography of international directories of foundations.

■ Gerding, S. K. and McKellar, P. H. (2006) *Grants for Libraries: A How-To-Do-It Manual*, New York: Neal-Schuman Publishers.

Like all the titles in the How-To-Do-It series, this is a practical guide to securing grants for your library. It covers the process from planning, to writing a proposal, to execution and has a very good chapter on sources of funding. The book also includes a CD-ROM with templates and the authors have a website that updates funding sources at *http://librarygrants.blogspot.com*

- The Taft Group (2006) *The Big Book of Library Grant Money 2006: Profiles of Private and Corporate Foundations and Direct Corporate Givers Receptive to Library Grant Proposals*, Chicago: American Library Association.

As the title suggests, this is a listing of nearly 2,400 private and corporate foundations that have given to libraries or have indicated an interest in doing so. It compiles a wealth of information on each organisation, including portfolio information, analysis of current and past projects, and full contact information.

Sources of funding

- Action on Disability and Development, Vallis House, 57 Vallis Road, Frome, Somerset BA11 3EG, UK; Tel: +44 (0)1373 473064; Fax: +44 (0)1373 452075; *http://www.add.org.uk*

ADD works with organisations of disabled people, primarily in less-developed countries, to help them improve their standard of living and advocate for equal rights.

- The Bill and Melinda Gates Foundation, PO Box 23350, Seattle, WA 98102, USA; Tel: +1 206 709 3100; *www.gatesfoundation.org*

The Gates Foundation supports both US and international initiatives focused on providing access to information technology in public libraries.

- Christian Blind Mission, Nibelungenstraße 124, 64625 Bensheim, Germany; Tel: +49 6251 131 392; Fax: +49 6251 131 338; *http://www.cbm.org*

CBM is an international development agency for people with disabilities. It supports the provision of services to persons with visual disabilities as well as people with other disabilities in more than 1,000 projects in 113 developing countries.

- The FORCE Foundation, Huijgensstraat 9a, 2515 BD The Hague, Netherlands; Tel: +31 (0)70 3097698 *http://www.force-worldwide.org*

The FORCE Foundation helps blind and visually impaired children and adults in developing countries to improve their lives by providing access to information. They have a long history of supporting libraries in this mission.

- Handicap-International, 14, Avenue Berthelot, 69361 Lyon cedex 07, France; Tel: + 33 (0)4 78 69 79 79; Fax: + 33 (0)4 78 69 79 94; *http://www.handicap-international .org*

Handicap-International is an international nonprofit organisation working in over 50 countries to help people coping with disabling situations. Headquartered in France, they have offices in the UK, Germany, Luxembourg, Switzerland, Canada and the USA.

- The Institute for Museum and Library Services, 1800 M Street NW, 9th Floor, Washington, DC 20036–5802, USA; Tel: +1 202 653 4657; Fax: 202 653 4600; *www.imls.gov*

An independent grant-making agency of the US government, it provides federal grants for library services on a range of issues and topics. The IMLS also provides funds to state library associations to support the goals of the Library Services and Technology Act, a primary source of funding for improving access in American libraries.

■ Leonard Cheshire International, 30 Millbank, London, SW1P 4QD UK; Tel: +44 (0)20 7802 8224; Fax: +44 (0)20 7802 8275; *http://www.lcint.org.uk/*

Leonard Cheshire International is the international arm of the UK registered charity, Leonard Cheshire, which is the largest provider of services for disabled people in the UK. The international work of Leonard Cheshire extends to 57 countries worldwide and aims to improve the quality of life for disabled people and their families.

■ The Open Society Institute, 400 West 59th Street, New York, NY 10019, USA; Tel: +1 212 548 0600; *www.soros .org/initiatives/information*

Through their Information Program Initiative, OSI aims to 'enhance the ability to access, exchange, and produce knowledge and information' for disadvantaged groups, especially in less-affluent parts of the world.

■ The Rotary Foundation, Rotary International, One Rotary Center, 1560 Sherman Ave., Evanston, IL 60201, USA; Tel: +1 847 866 3000; Fax: +1 847 328 8554 or +1 847 328 8281; *www.rotary.org*

Through local and district chapters, the Rotary Foundation administers a broad range of humanitarian and educational programmes and activities to help 'improve the human condition and advance the ultimate goal of world peace'.

■ United Nations Voluntary Fund on Disability: Secretariat for the Convention on the Rights of Persons with

Disabilities, Two United Nations Plaza, DC2–1372, New York, NY 10017, USA; Fax: +1 212 963 0111; *http://www.un.org/esa/socdev/enable/disunvf.htm*

The Voluntary Fund on Disability is the UN vehicle for providing support for people with disabilities. It supports both disability organisations and smaller projects designed to improve the lives of people with disabilities.

Bibliography

Abang, T. B. (1992) 'Special education in Nigeria', *International Journal of Disability, Comparative Educational Review* 27: 324–40.

Amato, I. (2006) 'Silent chemistry', *Chemical and Engineering News* 84(12): 53–6.

Andrich, R. (1999) *Assistive Technology Education for End Users: Guidelines for Trainers*, Milan: EUSTAT Telematics Applications Programme.

Arrue, M., Vigo, M. and Abascal, J. (2006) 'Architecture for personal web accessibility, computers helping people with special needs', Proceedings of ICCHP 2006: 10th International Conference on Computers, Helping People with Special Needs, University of Linz, 12–14 July, *Lecture Notes in Computer Science* 4061: 120–7.

Atinmo, M. I. (1979) 'Public and school library services to the physically handicapped in Nigeria: an evaluation', *International Library Review* 11(1): 471–9.

Atinmo, M. I. and Dawha, E. M. K. (1997) 'The reading needs of exceptional students and the dilemma of equity of access to information: a case study of the University of Ibadan', *The Exceptional Child: The Journal of the National Council for Exceptional Children* 1(2): 25–9.

Atkinson, M. T., Dhiensa, J. and Machin, C. H. C. (2006) 'Opening up access to online documents using essentiality tracks', Proceedings of the 2006 International

Cross-Disciplinary Workshop on Web Accessibility (W4A), Edinburgh, 22–3 May; New York: ACM Press; pp. 6–13.

Australian Bureau of Statistics (ABS) (1996) *Disability, Ageing and Carers, Australia Disability and Disabling Conditions 1993*, Canberra: AGPS.

Australian Bureau of Statistics (ABS) (1999) 'Activity patterns of people with a disability or who are principal carers', *Year Book Australia 1999*, Canberra: AGPS.

Australian Bureau of Statistics (ABS) (2000) *Disability and Long Term Health Conditions*, Canberra: AGPS.

Australian Bureau of Statistics (ABS) (2004) *Preliminary Findings of the 2003 Survey of Disability, Aging and Carers*, Canberra: AGPS; available at: *http://www.abs.gov.au/Ausstats* (accessed: 21 March 2006).

Australian Institute of Health and Welfare (AIHW) (2000) *Disability – National Picture*, available at: *http://www.aihw.gov.au/search.cfm/criteria/Disability* (accessed: 21 March 2006).

Australian Library and Information Association (ALIA) (2003) *Statement on Information Literacy for all Australians*, Canberra: ALIA; available at: *http://www.alia.org.au/policies/information.literacy.html* (accessed: 21 March 2006).

Bakare, C. A. (1992) 'Integration in education: the case of education for the handicapped children in Nigeria', *International Journal of Special Education* 7: 225–60.

Baum, C. M. (1998) 'Achieving effectiveness with a client centred approach: a person-environment interaction', in Gray, D. B., Quatrann, L. A. and Lieberman, M. L. (eds.) *Designing and Using Assistive Technology: The Human Perspective*, Baltimore, MD: Paul H. Brookes; pp. 137–47.

BBC (2006) 'Government sites fail web tests', available at: *http://news.bbc.co.uk/1/hi/technology/4853000.stm* (accessed 24 November 2006).

Braillecode.com (year unknown) 'Louis Braille: 6 dot Braille', available at: *http://www.braillecode.com/braille-alphabet.html* (accessed 24 November 2006).

Brooks, N. A. (1991) 'Users' responses to assistive devices for physical disability', *Social Science and Medicine* 32(12): 1417–24.

Bruce, C. S. (1997) *The Seven Faces of Information Literacy*, Adelaide: Auslib Press.

Carey, K. (2005) 'Accessibility: the current situation and new directions', *Ariadne* 44, available at: *http://www.ariadne.ac.uk/issue44/carey/* (accessed 28 November 2006).

Charles, S. (2005) 'Person first, disability second: disability awareness training in libraries' *Library Review* 54(8): 453–8.

Collins, J. (1994) 'Understanding the problems of being partially sighted', in Hogg, F.N. (ed.) *Looking ahead: a practical look at new developments in library and information services for visually impaired persons. Papers presented at the second international conference on library services to visually impaired persons, held at the University of Nottingham, 15–18 July,* Leicester: Ulverscroft.

Cook, A. M. and Hussey, S. M. (1995) *Assistive Technologies: Principles and Practice.* St Louis, MO: Mosby.

COST 219 bis (2001) *Bridging the Gap? Access to Telecommunications for All People*, Switzerland: Commission of European Communities; available at *http://www.tiresias.org/phoneability/bridging_the_gap/* (accessed 28 November 2006).

Covington, G. A. (1998) 'Cultural and environmental barriers to assistive technology', In Gray, D. B., Quatrann, L. A. and Lieberman, M. L. (eds) *Designing and Using Assistive Technology: The Human Perspective*, Baltimore, MD: Paul H. Brookes; pp. 77–88.

Cowan, D. M. and Turner-Smith, A. R. (1999), 'The users' perspective on the provision of electronic assistive technology: equipped for life?', *British Journal of Occupational Therapy* 62(1): 2–6.

Crouse, S. F. M. (2004) 'The academic support needs of students with impairments at three higher education institutions', *South African Journal of Higher Education* 18(1): 228–51.

DAISY Consortium (2006) 'About the DAISY Consortium', available at: *http://www.daisy.org/about_us/default.asp* (accessed 24 November 2006).

Danlami, B. (2000) 'Resource sharing among institutions and libraries serving the blind in Nigeria', *Development and Education* 39: 13–18.

Day, J. M. (1999) 'Online deafness and deaf culture information resources', *Education Libraries* 23(1): 5–8.

Day, J. M. and International Federation of Library Associations and Institutions (2000) *Guidelines for Library Services to Deaf People*, The Hague: IFLA Headquarters.

De Gasperi, M. and Valentino C. (2003) 'Library services for users with motor, visual and hearing disabilities: theory and practice', *Bollettino AIB* 43(4): 463–71.

Deines-Jones, C. (1999) 'Training professional and support staff members' in McNulty, T. (ed.) *Accessible Libraries on Campus: A Practical Guide for the Creation of Disability-Friendly Libraries*, Chicago, IL: American Library Association, Association of College and Research Libraries.

Deines-Jones, C. and Van Fleet, C. (1995) *Preparing Staff to Serve Patrons with Disabilities: A How-to-do-it Manual*, New York, Neal-Schuman.

Dhiensa, J., Machin, C., Smith, F. and Stone, R. (2005) 'Optimizing the user environment: leading towards an accessible and usable experience', paper presented at the

Accessible Design in the Digital World Conference, Dundee, 23–5 August.

Dotless Braille (year unknown) 'Five-minute introduction to Braille', available at: *http://www.dotlessbraille.org/Five.htm* (accessed 24 November 2006).

Emiliani, P. L. (1997) 'Information technology, telecommunications and disability: an approach towards integration', *ERCIM News* 28 (January): 11–13.

Forrest, M. E. S. (2006) 'Towards an accessible academic library: using the *IFLA Checklist*', *IFLA Journal* 32(1): 13–18.

Goddard, M. L. and Association of Specialized and Cooperative Library Agencies (1996) *Guidelines for Library and Information Services for the American Deaf Community*, Chicago, IL: Association of Specialized and Cooperative Library Agencies, American Library Association.

Galvin, J. C. (1997) 'Assistive technology: federal policy and practice since 1982', *Technology and Disability* 6: 3–15.

Goggin, G. and Newell, C. (2003) *Digital Disability: the Social Construction of Disability in New Media*, Lanham, MD: Rowman and Littlefield Publishers.

Hannah, K. (2003) 'Developing accessible library services', *Library + Information Update* 2(11): 50–2.

Harrington, T. R. (1998) 'The deaf collection at the Gallaudet University Library', *Education Libraries* 22(3): 3–12.

Harris, C. and Oppenheim, C. (2003) 'The provision of library services for visually impaired students in UK further education libraries in response to the Special Educational Needs and Disability Act (SENDA)' *Journal of Librarianship and Information Science* 35: 243–57.

Hearing Loss Association of America (2006) 'Facts on hearing loss', available at: *http://www.hearingloss.org/learn/factsheets.asp* (accessed 28 November 2006).

Hedge, A. (2006) 'Cutaneous displays', available at: *http://ergo.human.cornell.edu/studentdownloads/DEA32 5pdfs/idcutaneous.pdf* (accessed 24 November 2006).

Hocking, C. (1999) 'Function or feelings: factors in abandonment of assistive devices', *Technology and Disability* 11(1/2): 3–11.

Iaccarino, G., Malandrino, D. and Scarano, V. (2006) 'Personalizable edge services for web accessibility', Proceedings of the 2006 International Cross-Disciplinary Workshop on Web Accessibility (W4A), Edinburgh, 22–3 May; New York: ACM Press; pp. 23–32.

IBM (2005) 'Solution scenarios for the use of ViaScribe and CaptionMeNow: a best-of-breed captioning solution', available at: *http://www.cita.uiuc.edu/presentations/ 2006-02-16-ibm/ViaScribeWhitePaper.doc* (accessed 28 November 2006).

Ihunnah, A. C. (1984) 'The status of special education in a developing country: Nigeria' unpublished doctoral dissertation, Virginia Polytechnic Institute and State University, Blacksburg, VA.

James, A. and Litterick, I. (2004) 'Dyslexia friendly libraries' (updated July 2006), available at: *http://www .dyslexic.com/library.htm* (accessed 24 November 2006).

Johnstone, J. (2005) 'Employment of disabled persons in the academic library environment', *Australian Library Journal* 54(2): 156–63.

Jones, A. and Tedd, L. A. (2003) 'Provision of electronic information services for the visually impaired: an overview with case studies from three institutions within the University of Wales', *Journal of Librarianship and Information Science* 35(2): 105–13.

Keating, E. and Mirus, G. (2003) 'American Sign Language in virtual space: interactions between deaf users of computer-mediated video communication and the impact of technology on language practices', *Language in Society* 32(5): 693–714.

Lajoie, L. (2003) 'Embracing the silence', *School Library Journal* 49(8): 43.

Lockyer, S., Creaser, C. and Davies, J. E. (2005) *Availability of Accessible Publications*, Loughborough: LISU. Department of Information Science LISU Occasional Paper no. 35, available at: *http://www.lboro.ac.uk/departments/dils/lisu/downloads/op35.pdf* (accessed 24 November 2006).

Lupton, D. and Seymour, W. (2000) 'Technology, selfhood and disability', *Social Science and Medicine* 50(12): 1851–62.

MacMillan, K. (2004) 'Hands-on collection building', *School Library Journal* 50(3): 46–7.

Marks, K. S. (2005) 'Deaf patrons in the rural library: the benefits of community networks', *Bookmobile and Outreach Services* 8(2): 7–19.

Mates, B. T. (2000) *Adaptive Technology for the Internet: Making Electronic Resources Accessible to All*, Chicago, IL: ALA Editions, American Library Association.

Mazrui, J. (2005) 'What's in a PDF? The challenges of the popular Portable Document Format', available at: *http://www.afb.org/AFBPress/pub.asp?DocID=aw060604* (accessed 24 November 2006).

Mba, P. O. (2000) *Fundamentals of Special Education and Vocational Rehabilitation*, Ibadan: Codat Publishers.

McCaffrey, M. (2004) 'The missing link', *School Library Journal* 50(9): 48–9.

McNulty, Tom (ed.) (1999) *Accessible Libraries on Campus: A Practical Guide for the Creation of Disability-Friendly Libraries*, Chicago, IL: American Library Association; Association of College and Research Libraries.

McQuigg, K. (2003) 'Are the deaf a disabled group, or a linguistic minority? Issues for librarians in Victoria's public libraries', *Australian Library Journal* 52(4): 367–77.

Monaghan, L. F., Schmaling, C., Nakamura, K. and Turner, G. H. (eds) (2003) *Many Ways to be Deaf: International Variation in Deaf Communities*, Washington, DC: Gallaudet University Press.

Mendis, P. (1989) 'Education of personnel: the key to successful community based rehabilitation', In Helander, E., Mendis, P., Nelson, G. and Goerdt, A. *Training in the Community for People with Disabilities*, Geneva: WHO.

National Technical Institute for the Deaf, Rochester Institute of Technology (2006) 'Hearing loss', available from: *http://www.ntid.rit.edu/media/hearing_loss.php* (accessed 13 March 2006).

Nguyen, T., R. Garrett, B., Downing, A., Walker, L. and Hobbs, D. (2004) 'Research into telecommunications options for people with physical disabilities', ARATA 2004 National Conference, Melbourne, 2–4 June.

Noland, A. (2003) 'How Cleveland serves the deaf community' *Public Libraries* 42(1): 20–1.

North Carolina State University (1997) *The Principles of Universal Design (Version 2.0)*, Raleigh, NC: The Center for Universal Design.

Obiakor, F. E., Bragg, W. A. and Maltby, G. P. (1993) 'Placement of exceptional students in Nigeria and the United States of America', paper presented at the International Association of Special Education Third Biennial Conference, Vienna, 5 July.

Ochoggia, R. E. (2003) 'Persons with disability bill 2002 and its implications to the provision of library and information services to the visually handicapped persons in Kenyan learning institutions', *University of Dar es Salaam Library Journal* 5(1): 24–33.

Oluigbo, E. C. (1986) *Statistics of Special Education Development in Nigeria, 1986: A Case Study*, Lagos: Federal Ministry of Education.

Oluigbo, E. C. (1990) *National Curriculum for the Mentally Retarded*, Lagos: Federal Ministry of Education.

Onwuegbu, O. L. (1977) 'The Nigerian culture: its perception and treatment of the handicapped', unpublished essays, Federal Advanced Teachers' College for Special Education, Oyo, Oyo State, Nigeria.

Pell, S. D., Gillies, R. M. and Carss, M. (1999) 'Use of technology by people with physical disabilities in Australia', *Disability and Rehabilitation* 21: 56–61.

Peters, S. J. (2003) 'Inclusive education: achieving education for all by including those with disabilities and special needs', Prepared for the Disability Group, Human Development Network of The World Bank; available at: *http://siteresources.worldbank.org/DISABILITY/Resources/Education/Inclusive_Education_En.pdf* (accessed 28 November 2006).

Peters, T. and Bell, L. (2006) 'Accessible IT: hello IM, goodbye TTY', *Computers in Libraries* 26(5): 18–21.

Pinfield, S. (2001) 'The changing role of subject librarians in academic libraries', *Journal of Librarianship and Information Science* 33(1): 32–8.

Playforth, S. (2004) 'Inclusive library services for deaf people: an overview from the social model perspective', *Health Information and Libraries Journal* 21(Supplement 2): 54–7.

Rodriguez, R. and Reed, M. (2003) 'Our deaf family needs to read, too', *Public Libraries* 42(1): 38–41.

Rubin, R. J. and Association of Specialized and Cooperative Library Agencies (2001) *Planning for Library Services to People with Disabilities*, Chicago, IL: Association of Specialized and Cooperative Library Agencies.

Runhare, T. (2004) 'Provision of equal education for students with disabilities at tertiary institutions in Zimbabwe: prospects and barriers', *Journal of Social Development in Africa* 19(1): 151–67.

Sataloff, R. T. and Sataloff, J. (2005) *Hearing Loss*, New York: Taylor and Francis.

Scherer, M. J. (2000) *Living in the State of Stuck: How Technology Impacts the Lives of People with Disabilities* (3rd edn), Cambridge, MA: Brookline Books.

Seiler, R. J., Seiler, A. M. and Ireland, J. M. (1997) 'Enhancing Internet access for people with disabilities', Proceedings of the 7th International World Wide Web Conference, Santa Clara, CA, 7–11 April.

Shearman, C. (1999) 'Local connection: making the Net work for people and communities', Community Networking Conference 'Engaging Regionalism', Ballarat, Victoria, 29 September – 1 October.

Sheldon, A. (2003) 'Changing technology', in Swain, J., French, S., Barnes, C. and Thomas, C. (eds) *Disabling Barriers – Enabling Environments*, London: Sage; pp. 155–60.

Smith, G. (2003) 'Why we need an assistive technology policy', *Link Magazine* 12(2): 20.

Stephanidis, C. and Emiliani, P. L. (1999) '"Connecting" to the information society: a European perspective', *Technology and Disability* 10: 21–44.

UK Disability Rights Commission (2004) 'Formal investigation report: web accessibility', available at: *http://www.drc-gb.org/library/website_accessibility_guidance/formal_investigation_report_w.aspx* (accessed 24 November 2006).

UNESCO (2005a) 'Information for All Programme: Thematic Debate on Information Literacy', The Bureau of the UNESCO's Intergovernmental Council for the

Information for All Programme (IFAP) Meeting, Paris, 5 April; available at: *http://portal.unesco.org/ci/en/ev .phpURL_ID=19621&URL_DO=DO_TOPIC&URL_ SECTION=201.html* (accessed 22 March 2006).

UNESCO (2005b) *Education for All Monitoring Report 2005: The Quality Imperative*, Paris: UNESCO.

Vanderheiden, G. C. (1998) 'Universal design and assistive technology in communication and information technologies: alternatives or compliments?', *Assistive Technology* 10: 29–36.

Vincent, C. and Morin, G. L. (1999) 'Utilizing assistive devices: comparison of the American model with the reality of the needs of Quebec', *Canadian Journal of Occupational Therapy* 66(2): 92–101.

Werle, M. (2003) 'Challenge your library to serve challenged individuals', *Public Libraries* 42(1): 16–17.

Williamson, K., Schauder, D. and Bow, A. (2000) 'Information seeking by blind and sight impaired citizens: an ecological study' *Information Research* 5(4); available at: *http://informationr.net/ir/5-4/paper79.html* (accessed 19 December 2006).

Wirz, S. and Meikle, S. (2005) 'Breaking barriers: Building access for disabled people', *Insights* 55 (May); available at: *http://www.id21.org/insights/insights55/insights-iss55-art00.html* (accessed 28 November 2006).

World Bank (2006) 'Disability: data and statistics', available at: *http://web.worldbank.org/WBSITE/EXTERNAL/ TOPICS/EXTSOCIALPROTECTION/EXTDISABILITY/ 0,,contentMDK:20196542~menuPK:282717~pagePK: 148956~piPK:216618~theSitePK:282699,00.html* (accessed 28 November 2006).

World Health Organization (1997) *International Classification System of Impairments, Activities and Participation* (ICIDH), Geneva: WHO.

World Health Organization (2005) 'Deafness and hearing impairment', fact sheet no. 300, available from: *http://www.who.int/mediacentre/factsheets/fs300/en/print.html* (accessed 15 March 2006).

World Health Organization (2006) 'CBR: A strategy for rehabilitation, equalization of opportunities, poverty reduction and social inclusion of people with disabilities: Joint position paper 2004'; available at: *http://www.ilo.org/public/english/employment/skills/download/jointpaper.pdf* (accessed 28 November 2006).

World Wide Web Consortium (W3C) (1999) 'Web content accessibility guidelines', available at: *http://www.w3.org/TR/WCAG10/* (accessed 24 November 2006).

Index